THE TIMES

The Games

Great Britain's finest sporting hour

HarperSport
An Imprint of HarperCollins*Publishers*

HarperSport
An imprint of HarperCollins*Publishers*
77–85 Fulham Palace Road,
Hammersmith, London W6 8JB

www.harpercollins.co.uk

First published by HarperCollins*Publishers* 2012

1 3 5 7 9 10 8 6 4 2

Design & Art Direction: Design by St

A catalogue record of this book is available from the British Library.

ISBN 978-0-00-750867-9

Printed and bound in Italy by L.E.G.O. S.p.A.

Contents

Introduction
Simon Barnes

LONDON WAS its usual cranky self. If there was anything unusual in the air, it served only as an opportunity for whinging; London, being old and somewhat stiff in its joints, has long believed that grumbling is a basic human right. Signal failures on the tubes, intrusive, unfair Olympic lanes on the roads, the influx of over-excited foreigners in curious patriotic garments and the continuing bloody awful weather: no good could come of it.

I travelled to the Olympic Park in just such a London on July 27. I travelled back to my hotel through an enchanted city at the heart of a magical land: Oz, Utopia, Erewhon, Narnia, Camelot, the Never Never Land, the country of the Houyhnhnms, the land at the end of the rainbow, the island where dreams come true, a brave new world, an island full of sweet sounds that give delight and hurt not. Even the weather wasn't too bad.

And there, the following morning, I discovered that I had helped to write not *The Times of London* but *The Times of the Emerald City*: a newspaper utterly changed to reflect these changing times, one that told not of war and horror and disaster but of the dawning of a period of magic. The paper was now wrapped in a single vast, beautiful photograph. The times were beautiful: *The Times* was beautiful. I set off for Greenwich Park and the horses.

What sorcery could work such a transformation? Love, obviously: only and obviously love. London had spent seven years being wooed by the Olympic Games and had been difficult to please, seeing only the defects of a too-ardent suitor. Seven years had passed since London was awarded the Games: seven years of bitching and moaning and refusing to see anything good, save the grudging admission that the 100 metres might be quite interesting. For the lucky bastards who had tickets, anyway.

Overnight everything changed. After this ardent but one-sided courtship, London and Britain fell without warning, fell like a ton of bricks – and the next 16 days were full of the euphoria of love requited. Each day was a day of fresh wonders: each day that followed was filled with the certainty of greater wonders to follow. The only thing that was better than yesterday was the still greater glory of today.

There is a terrible thing called disaster-shock that affects the victims of nightmarish occurrences: a complete overwhelming of the senses and the will. Something of the exact opposite affected those of us who were at the centre of these extraordinary 17 days. As one impossible day followed another, an increasing sense of shock worked its way through the members of Team Times. Many of us were

'Each day was a day of fresh wonders: each day that followed was filled with the certainty of greater wonders to follow. The only thing that was better than yesterday was the still greater glory of today.'

FRIDAY JULY 27 2012 | THETIMES.CO.UK | NO 70636

THE TIMES

MAX 28C, MIN 8C

OF LONDON

£1

SOUVENIR EDITION

'THE IMPORTANT THING IN THE OLYMPIC GAMES IS NOT WINNING BUT TAKING PART. THE ESSENTIAL THING IN LIFE IS NOT CONQUERING BUT FIGHTING WELL'

BARON PIERRE DE COUBERTIN
FOUNDER OF THE MODERN OLYMPICS

LET THE GAMES BEGIN

'BE NOT AFEARD; THE ISLE IS FULL OF NOISES, SOUNDS AND SWEET AIRS, THAT GIVE DELIGHT AND HURT NOT. SOMETIMES A THOUSAND TWANGLING INSTRUMENTS WILL HUM ABOUT MINE EARS, AND SOMETIME VOICES THAT, IF I THEN HAD WAKED AFTER LONG SLEEP, WILL MAKE ME SLEEP AGAIN; AND THEN, IN DREAMING, THE CLOUDS METHOUGHT WOULD OPEN AND SHOW RICHES READY TO DROP UPON ME, THAT WHEN I WAKED I CRIED TO DREAM AGAIN.'
WILLIAM SHAKESPEARE
THE TEMPEST | ACT III, SCENE 2
THE TIMES
OF LONDON
£1.50
SOUVENIR EDITION
A FLYING START

THE TIMES
OF LONDON
£1.50
SOUVENIR EDITION
THE GREATEST SHOW

THE TIMES
OF LONDON
SOUVENIR EDITION
£1
NOW SERVING
BORIS JOHNSON
BEIJING 2008

THE TIMES
OF LONDON
SOUVENIR EDITION
£1
MOD RULE
'THERE WAS A SLIGHT MELANCHOLY ON THE PODIUM. NOTHING WILL TOP THAT NOW. I'M CERTAINLY GOING TO GET A BIT DRUNK TONIGHT'
BRADLEY WIGGINS
GOLD MEDALLIST | MEN'S TIME TRIAL
BRITAIN'S MOST DECORATED OLYMPIAN

THE TIMES
ROCKET MAN

'WHEN IT COMES TO BUSINESS I KNOW WHAT I NEED TO DO, I HAVE A GREAT TALENT'
USAIN BOLT
THE TIMES
OF LONDON
SOUVENIR EDITION
£1
LIGHTNING STRIKE

'FLOAT LIKE A BUTTERFLY, STING LIKE A BEE. HIS HANDS CAN'T HIT WHAT HIS EYES CAN'T SEE'
MUHAMMAD ALI
THE TIMES
OF LONDON
SOUVENIR EDITION
£1
THE RIGHT STUFF

THE TIMES
OF LONDON
£1
'AT HIS BEST, EVERYONE ELSE AT THEIR BEST, HE WINS EVERY TIME. HE'S THAT GOOD'
MICHAEL JOHNSON
ON USAIN BOLT
COOL RUNNINGS

THE TIMES
OF LONDON
SOUVENIR EDITION
£1
ELIZABETH THE SECOND
'IT IS THE MOST SPECIAL THING I'VE EVER EXPERIENCED. IT'S SO CRAZY AND INSPIRING. I DIDN'T EVEN FEEL MY LEGS'

THE TIMES
OF LONDON
SOUVENIR EDITION
£1
THE HISTORY BOYS
'STAY IN THE ZONE, GET THE JOB DONE'

THE TIMES
£1
London 2012
GBR
'THERE IS NOTHING — ABSOLUTELY NOTHING — HALF SO MUCH WORTH DOING AS SIMPLY MESSING ABOUT IN BOATS'
RULING THE WAVES

THE TIMES
OF LONDON
SOUVENIR EDITION
£1.50
THE PURSUIT OF EXCELLENCE

THE TIMES
OF LONDON
SOUVENIR EDITION
£1
OLYMPIC GAMES
29 JULY 1948 14 AUGUST
LONDON
BRIDLED JOY

THE TIMES
OF LONDON
SOUVENIR EDITION
THE FLAG BEARER

THE TIMES
OF LONDON
SOUVENIR EDITION
£1.50
'THEY COMPETE TO SEE WHICH COUNTRY IN THE WORLD IS BEST AT SPLASHING ABOUT. IT'S SO HUMAN. SO REAL. SUCH A TIMELY THING TO BE DOING IN AUGUST'
COSTUME DRAMA

THE TIMES
OF LONDON
SOUVENIR EDITION
'THE SPIRIT OF THE OLYMPIC GAMES, WHICH HAS TARRIED HERE AWHILE, SETS FORTH ONCE MORE. MAY IT PROSPER THROUGHOUT THE WORLD, SAFE IN THE KEEPING OF ALL THOSE WHO HAVE FELT ITS IMPULSE IN THIS GREAT FESTIVAL OF SPORT'
THE ROAD TO RIO

staying at the Hotel Russell in Bloomsbury, from where we could cross the road to catch buses (in those suddenly quite acceptable Olympic lanes) to all the Olympic venues. We had no organised social life and there was no carousing, for there was no time, but occasionally we would meet up by accident, sometimes in twos and threes, sometimes in spontaneous groups, and have a drink or a plate of not terribly demanding food at the next-door Italian.

And always in this mood of disbelief, this strange feeling of being in a place and a time in which all the normal rules had been suspended. We were all a little more affectionate to each other than normal. We found ourselves talking more openly than is usual among colleagues: about our own lives, about our feelings, about what we were experiencing, about what we were a part of.

We were journalists stripped of the carapace of professional cynicism. We didn't feel like dispassionate observers, refined out of existence, paring our fingernails, reporting on the events with detached calm. We felt part of a miracle. There was an unaccustomed warmth in what we wrote. There was also a sense of risk: don't ever be afraid of going big. Not while it still lasts.

We were, after all, on the biggest story of our lives. We were writing about a Home Games: none of us will do that again. This was the moment to play your big shots, to play the innings of your life. It was a feeling that gave us a certain empathy with the athletes. True, we hadn't worked for four years with nothing else in view but one single day: but as we sought to raise our own games to the highest possible level, we got the general idea.

It was astonishing to get up every morning and pick up *The Times*, shoved brusquely under the hotel door, and behold a thing of beauty. Every day of the Games was a day out of the common run of things: every day brought a newspaper to match.

A journalist, like any other employee, is more inclined to whinge about their employer than to lavish praise upon them (see paragraph one). But for this magical period, that daily first sight of the newspaper was a thing to glory in. And once you got past the lovely wrap, the newspaper was all about us: no political knavery, no international horror could shove sport – silly old trivial old ridiculous old sport – off the front pages nor cause the diminution of the 40-page Olympic pull-out.

We had dressage on the front page of *The Times*. That day, I felt like retiring at once from all horse-writing, for surely I will never top that. *The Times* afternoon editorial conference was interrupted not once but twice so that the *Times'* high-ups could watch Charlotte Dujardin and Valegro doing their stuff in the dressage arena.

That's what it was like at *The Times*: that's what it was like for the entire country. Every day we fell in love with a new way in which humans sought glory and perfection. The country was lit up with passage and piaffe, split-times, heptathlon points, pommel-horse dismounts, stroke-rates, jumping penalties, the dive tariff, double trap, the exact worth of a kick in the crotch at taekwondo, the difference between snatch and clean-and-jerk, the problem of controlling pulse and respiration in modern pentathlon.

And then there was Usain Bolt, who performed the most essential job of all at the London Olympic Games. The glory of Bolt has nothing to do with nationality. Bolt's scintillating run in the 100 metres reminded Britain that it wasn't just about us: that this great festival was an international thing, a celebration not of London and Britain but of brilliant individual humans and of all humanity.

We were not the winners: we were the hosts. We weren't conquering the world: we were the grateful recipients of the world's blessing. On the night of the 100 metres final, I wrote the splash – jargon for the front-page lead story – in the stadium and the following morning the nation was still rapt and *The Times* was wrapped in the wonder of Bolt.

For the rest: well, it's all in here, as told by me and my colleagues, in words and in pictures. Much of the glory of the Games was in women: and day after day we celebrated women not for their winsomeness but for their strength of body and of mind, and if I had my pick of what sporting legacy we want from these Games, it's that women and women's sport get higher up the sporting agenda.

I shall close here with a journalist's story. I was back in Greenwich Park and had just finished 1,200 words on the eventers and the British silver medal for the sports pages. I now had to write a further 800 words on Mary King, the British heroine, who, aged 51, had set the tone for the British effort. This was for page three, on the news pages. And I was at a loss.

I've known Mary for years: brilliant, delightful, courageous, ever-so-slightly barking. But I wasn't sure where to start this latest tale, and so I took a walk outside, away from the tensions of the press-room to see if I could find an opening paragraph – an intro, in the jargon – in the colonnade outside. And found Mary. She was passing by, and her smile was like a supernova. So instead of wheedling a quote from her, as journalistic practice demanded, I told her she was wonderful and kissed her. 'Feel my medal,' Mary said. It was a great solid thing, a chunk of metal that said something serious about glory and its pursuit.

That kiss and the fondling of the medal gave me an intro, a free and generous gift from the gods of sportswriting, and it was a moment that encapsulated everything that was perfect about the London Olympic Games of 2012. It was a blessed time: and we were there. If any of that sense of being blessed has survived in the words and the pictures that follow, we have given a true account of the most extraordinary period of all of our professional careers.

'This great festival was an international thing, a celebration not of London and Britain but of brilliant individual humans and of all humanity.'

'THE SPIRIT OF THE OLYMPIC GAMES, WHICH HAS TARRIED HERE AWHILE, SETS FORTH ONCE MORE. MAY IT PROSPER THROUGHOUT THE WORLD, SAFE IN THE KEEPING OF ALL THOSE WHO HAVE FELT ITS IMPULSE IN THIS GREAT FESTIVAL OF SPORT'

LORD BURGHLEY,
ORGANISING COMMITTEE CHAIRMAN,
LONDON OLYMPICS 1948

THE TIMES

MAX 25C, MIN 11C

OF LONDON

£1

SOUVENIR EDITION

LAP OF HONOUR

THE LONDON OLYMPIC STADIUM, HOST OVER THE PAST TWO WEEKS TO WORLD RECORDS, PERSONAL TRIUMPHS AND THE GREATEST DRAMA, SEES OFF THE GAMES WITH AN ELECTRIFYING CLOSING CEREMONY.

27.07.12

London 2012 Olympic Games

Day 1

1

Friday, July 27: London opens up

When Danny Boyle unveiled his vision for the opening ceremony of the London Olympics in June, there were those who greeted the announcement with something between a sly smirk and an outright guffaw.

There was no shortage of columnists, commentators, self-appointed online experts and harrumphing letter-writers pouring scorn on the plans. Sheep? Morris dancers? Village cricket? Didn't Boyle know that most of us live in cities and do not pine for some long-lost and largely imagined rural idyll? It would be a toe-curling embarrassment and confirm the suspicions of the world that this is a land trapped in a cycle of nostalgia.

It was a ceremony that only a filmmaker could conceive. From a pastoral idyll rose smoking towers and clanking machinery, while brave volunteers climbed chimneys or stripped away the green fields.

'It is hard to remember any public event that so united the country in admiration as the opening ceremony of the 2012 Olympic Games.'

At a little after 10pm on Friday July 27, as Boyle's 'Isles of Wonder' spectacular came to its breathtaking end, no one was laughing, unless it was Boyle allowing himself a grin of satisfaction at having pulled off such a spectacular coup with such utter brilliance.

It is hard to remember any public event that so united the country in admiration as the opening ceremony of the 2012 Olympic Games. Yes, there were wild flowers, milkmaids and a thatched croft, but there was also an extraordinary recreation of the birth of the Industrial Revolution (complete with Sir Kenneth Branagh dressed as Isambard Kingdom Brunel reading lines from *The Tempest*), a tribute to Britain's contribution to children's literature, featuring J. K. Rowling and 32 floating Mary Poppinses, and a moving, stunningly choreographed celebration of the NHS.

Right: In a spectacular, symbolic gesture, out of the darkness the Olympic rings rose up from around the stadium to forge together in a shower of golden fireworks.

After a series of elaborately choreographed musical routines to celebrate the best of Britain, representatives from each competing nation came together to create the cauldron which would hold the flame for the duration of the Games.

And that is not to mention Mr Bean's contribution to the *Chariots of Fire* theme and the showstopping appearance of the Queen making her acting debut alongside James Bond in what will remain without question the defining image of the start of London 2012.

The much-debated issue of who would light the flame was handled with equal flair – from David Beckham's Bond-like speedboat dash down the Thames from the Tower of London, to the handover to Sir Steve Redgrave to the final decision to leave the lighting to seven young British athletes. Thomas Heatherwick's innovative design for the cauldron drew much praise, too.

Perhaps the thought that featured most in the reviews and reflections about the ceremony afterwards was how Boyle's event had showed a nation at last relaxed about its place in the world, comfortable with its 21st-century multicultural identity and, crucially, able to laugh at itself as much as celebrate its achievements. It was the perfect launch.

28.07.12
London 2012 Olympic Games
Day 2

Medals won by Team GB
Gold 0
Silver 0
Bronze 0

2

Men's cycling team
Road race

Right: The hopes of a British gold on the first full day of Olympic competition were not to be fulfilled in the men's road race.
Overleaf: Thousands of spectators lined the route of the men's road race, from Buckingham Palace to the green hills of Surrey

YOU CAN choreograph an opening ceremony but not a 250km road race, as Mark Cavendish and his valiant team-mates were forced to accept when hopes of a first home gold medal at London 2012 ended in crushing disappointment.

On the first official day of competition, five hours of brutally hard work, and rising, beguiling hope, were destroyed in the final 45 minutes as the plan of delivering Cavendish to a triumphant sprint up The Mall was undone by an uncooperative gang of 30 breakaway riders.

The men's road race did not have the victor a home nation craved – and the result probably did not please the IOC or UCI either as Alexander Vinokourov beat Rigoberto Uran in the final sprint to claim the gold medal. Vinokourov is a troubling blast from cycling's past, an alleged ex-doper who has never confessed.

Cavendish trailed in 40 seconds later, 28 places further back than he had dared to dream, complaining angrily about the lack of support given to his team-mates by other nations in the 60kmph pursuit back into London. 'We expected teams to come and chase at the end with us,' he said. 'We controlled it with four guys for 250km and we couldn't do more. We are human beings.'

He might have had a point about Germany, who did little more than briefly loan Tony Martin to help at the front, but it was hardly a surprise that so many conspired against Britain and Cavendish.

Team GB had managed to exert an iron control of the race on a flatter course, and with more riders, at the World Championships in Copenhagen last year. But here? 'We had done five and a quarter hours on the front and we did not have that extra little bit,' David Millar said. 'What we needed was three fresh riders. When every other team is racing with the sole tactic to thrash our race up, it's very hard to do it. It was their job to try and derail us, which they did. To be fair, it was a slim chance to pull it off.'

For all his success, Cavendish remains without an Olympic medal, having trailed way down the field in the Madison in Beijing. Home expectations, soaring after Bradley Wiggins' victory in the Tour de France, probably did not reflect the fiendish difficulty of the task ahead of Britain. The crowds were enormous, experienced riders saying that they had never known an atmosphere like it.

This was a tantalising race throughout, with the first breakaway as soon as the riders left Richmond Park on the way out of London. The gap, dangerously, extended beyond six minutes.

Riding at the front of the main peloton throughout, Wiggins, Chris Froome, Ian Stannard and Millar took turns to lead the pursuit as rivals, including Vincenzo Nibali, launched fresh attacks.

The British effort was colossal but it came at a costly price. Two breakaway groups containing 32 riders formed as the race came off Box Hill for the ninth and final time. The gap was never much more than a minute but it was a high-class field ahead of a tiring Team GB.

There was more drama as the race returned to Richmond Park. Fabian Cancellara led the riders into a tight corner at Richmond Gate but misjudged the bend, crashing into a barrier. In the confusion, the group split up and Vinokourov and Uran established a lead which they took into The Mall where the Colombian was caught napping by his victorious rival in the last 300 metres.

Eight seconds behind the leaders, Alexander Kristoff, the Norwegian, won the sprint for bronze from a group including Taylor Phinney and Stuart O'Grady.

Cavendish finished with a half-flat tyre while his exhausted team-mates came home in dribs and drabs. 'I can be proud of how the lads rode today,' he said. 'I'm proud of my country as there was incredible support. The guys are spent. They have got nothing left in the tank. It's incredible to see that. To see what they gave for the cause.'
– *Matt Dickinson*

Louis Smith

Gymnastics

IF THERE were any doubt that home advantage or patriotic fervour can stretch the sinews that little bit more, or deepen the energy reserves, then the men's gymnastics team proved it with a spectacular display.

Britain were only good enough to send two gymnasts to Beijing, but on the first day of the competition in London the quintet upset China, the Olympic champions, to qualify for the final for the first time since 1924. A superb pommel horse by Louis Smith was the highlight. He finished almost 2.5 points ahead of China with a total of 272.420. The USA, in the other qualifying round, were the most impressive, tallying 275.342.

The British, meanwhile, could hardly contain their smiles – and, for Smith, a few tears. Smith's bronze on pommel horse four years ago was the country's first Olympic medal in 80 years, and this is the first time Britain qualified full men's and women's teams to the Olympics since the boycotted 1984 Games. Smith and three-time world champion Beth Tweddle have sparked a resurgence in this sport. They may not have Japan's style or the Americans' flash. But they are steady and solid, with a few flashes of brilliance thrown in – like Smith's pommel horse routine.

Most gymnasts simply pray to stay on the horse, looking as if they're trying to wrestle it to the ground as they work their way around the apparatus. But Smith is so smooth that he's almost hypnotic, swinging slowly and in perfect circles.

He had the consistency of a metronome as he worked on one pommel, his legs glued together, his rhythm never flagging. He finished with the flourish, his legs hitting the mat without moving an inch. As his team-mates whooped and clapped, Smith gave a big smile and exchanged a hand slap with Kristian Thomas, his team-mate.

When his score – a monstrous 15.8 – was announced, he began crying as the crowd roared.
– *Ed Hawkins*

POLICE

GREAT BRITAIN

Men's swimming
4 x 100 metres relay

Phelps recovered his form in the 4 x 100 metres relay, but even his heroic swim couldn't bring home gold for the team.

THE BATTLE of the American swimming supermen took a fascinating turn when they joined forces into a kind of superteam – and still could not bring the star of Beijing his first London Olympic gold medal.

In the men's 4 x 100 metres relay, it was Ryan Lochte, the man who would be king, whose hand slipped when reaching for the crown. Lochte has said that this is his year, and this was his chance to pull off some Phelpsian heroics. Earlier in the day he swam in the 200 metres freestyle heats and qualified second fastest. In the evening he swam the 200 metres semi-finals and came second to qualify for the final, and 80 minutes later he was lining up to swim the glory leg for the United States in the relay.

This was the kind of preposterous schedule that Phelps managed to pull off en route to his eight gold medals in Beijing. But Lochte could not match it, and in so doing, he managed to turn the gold medal that his team-mates had set him up to win into silver.

Phelps could not have done much more for the cause. In the relay, he started in the lead and simply extended it, and a similar job was done by Cullen Jones. When Lochte set off in pursuit of his second gold, he was given a lead of more than half a second. The Frenchman next to him, Yannick Agnel, however, was not interested in Lochte's reputation. His pursuit of the American was thrilling; he turned just behind him and then, in the last 25 metres, came sweeping past.
– Owen Slot

Ye Shiwen
400 metres individual medley

A WAVE OF incredulity had swept through the media seats even before Ye Shiwen had turned for the last time on her way to gold in the 400 metres individual medley.

A body length behind at the end of breaststroke, Ye, who took up swimming at the age of 6 after a kindergarten teacher spotted her big hands and directed her parents to the pool, powered past Elizabeth Beisel, of the United States, like a speedboat trouncing a tug.

Take any world-class 400 metres medley title race among women in recent years and the average homecoming 100 metres freestyle split is about 1 minute 2.00 seconds.

Lochte, Beisel's training partner at the University of Florida came home to gold in the men's 400 metre medley in 58.65, his last 50 metres in 29.10. Ye was timed at 58.68 for her closing 100 metres, last length 28.93, for a world record of 4:28.43, the first world record to fall to a woman since the ban on booster bodysuits in 2010.

Beisel's time, 4:31.27, would have been the best by a woman in a textile suit. Ye's team-mate, Li Xuanxu, was next in 4:32.91.

Among those locked out by sizeable margins were the former Olympic and world champions and Britain's Hannah Miley, the European and Commonwealth champion.

Ye skipped out of the water on her way to interviews, doping control and a warmdown in the side pool, as though she had just come from taking a dip in a hotel leisure pool.

'No way – what the hell was that?' shouted an American reporter. That was the sight of history: since women first arrived in the Olympic pool, none had ever swum the last length (or any other part) of a race faster than the winning man in the equivalent event.

Ye's off-the-chart speed at the end of an Olympic 400 metres medley final that made world-class athletes look dead in the water has put Chinese swimming back in the headlines, on the blogs and in the chatrooms of the world, but not always in a positive way.
– Craig Lord

Day 2 Round Up

SWIMMING
16-year-old schoolgirl Ye Shiwen surged to victory in the women's 400 metres medley. Her winning time of 4:28.43 smashed all records.

ARCHERY
Italy beat the United States by just one point to win gold at Lord's. South Korea beat Mexico to win the bronze medal. Team GB's archers were beaten by Ukraine in the first round.

FENCING
Great Britain were knocked out of the women's individual foil. The Republic of Korea competed with Italy in the semi-finals; Italy took gold, silver and bronze in the final results.

FOOTBALL
Japan drew with Sweden, Brazil beat New Zealand, and Canada won against South Africa on the third day of the women's group stages. Britain's women beat Cameroon 3–0.

JUDO
Sarah Menezes won a first Olympic gold medal for Brazil's women's team as she dethroned the reigning champion, Romania's Alina Dumitru.

SHOOTING
Gyi Siling shot to victory and won the first gold medal of the Games for China in the shooting event, while Jin Jongoh won gold for the Republic of Korea.

WEIGHTLIFTING
China won eight weightlifting gold medals at the Beijing Games four years ago and struck gold again in the opening event as Wang Mingjuan won the under-48kg women's event.

MEDAL TABLE

				T
1. CHINA	4	0	2	6
2. ITALY	2	2	1	5
3. USA	1	2	2	5
4. BRAZIL	1	1	1	3
5. SOUTH KOREA	1	1	1	3
GREAT BRITAIN	0	0	0	0

IN NUMBERS

Olympic sports

26

Disciplines

39

Medal events

302

29.07.12
London 2012 Olympic Games
Day 3

Medals won by Team GB
Gold 0
Silver 1
Bronze 1

3

Lizzie Armitstead
Women's road race

AFTER THE disappointment of the men's road race on Day 2, all eyes were on the women, waiting to see if they could do what the men could not. They did not disappoint. Their sterling effort meant they claimed Great Britain's first medal.

Lizzie Armitstead gave a breakthrough performance over 140km. To finish a bike length behind Marianne Vos was a triumph, even if Armitstead could not help wondering whether it might, just might, have been even more glorious in that sprint down The Mall in teeming rain. 'My only regret is that I didn't try to jump her earlier in the sprint,' Armitstead said. 'I was about to go when she went just ahead of me. I've replayed that sprint 15 times in my head already.'

Even on a day which began with thunder and pelting rain for long periods, this race could be chalked up as another triumph for the Olympics and especially for cycling. The crowds were huge considering the downpour. 'It was something that I will never forget,' Armitstead said. 'It was strange not to be able to hear yourself think.'

There was plenty to cheer. The race featured incessant attacks, led early on by the Dutch. And if none of them stuck until the decisive move prompted by Olga Zabelinskaya coming off the second, and final, lap of Box Hill, there was an unrelenting drama in the jostling. Emma Pooley, Armitstead's team-mate, rode brilliantly in support, either tracking breaks at the front or stretching the field with her own burst, as needed.

It was as well that Pooley was in such great form because Nicole Cooke, the defending Olympic champion, struggled to feature while Lucy Martin, picked to help Armitstead in a lead-out, was dropped behind as soon as the race hit Box Hill.

Vos, Armitstead, Zabelinskaya, of Russia, and Shelley Olds, of the United States, formed a powerful quartet, quickly establishing a 20-second lead in the downpour. In spreading grit across the road, the rain would also cause countless punctures – including a critical one for Olds as the breakaway quartet raced back towards London.

Suddenly there were three and a medal was guaranteed if they could stay ahead of the chasing pack. With an incentive to co-operate, Vos and Armitstead stretched the lead, with Zabelinskaya clinging on until the last couple of kilometres.

'Like a dream,' Armitstead said of the sensation of crossing the line. 'It's something you've worked at for four years and in a flash it's over.'

– Matt Dickinson

Rebecca Adlington

Women's 400 metres freestyle

OVER IN the Olympic Park, ladies' day continued for Team GB; bronze was not the colour she had dreamt of, but for Rebecca Adlington and her supporters it was no less well-received.

They may have turned down the temperature in the Aquatics Centre, but you still could feel an extraordinary warmth for Adlington when her Olympic 400 metres title was taken from her. For this was not so much a title lost as a medal won. And no, it was not gold, not of the hue that we associate with Adlington, not even a silver, but a triumph nevertheless.

So the repeat double is beyond her; that is now official. But although on Day 3 Adlington wrote a different kind of chapter in her extraordinary story, it was very much a tale of London, of a complicated love affair with the home Games crowd, and about how that relationship helped her drain the best of herself so she could deliver a medal.

When Adlington walked on to the pooldeck at 8.10pm for her final, the noise was shrill and loud, and all she could do was keep her head down. There is a lot tied up in this. She knew that half of the United Kingdom seemed to think she would win gold; that is simply what she does, turn up and win. Yet in her mind, she thought that she had no chance. Camille Muffat, the French girl, was simply swimming too well.

Overwhelmed, Adlington set about delivering one of her great performances. In the morning, in her heat, she had done the opposite, she had gone out fast and faded to such an extent that she qualified in eighth. So she went into the final not knowing what she had left in her. Even on her Twitter feed, she said: 'Not expecting anything tonight. All I can do is my best.'

Her best was pretty impressive. It was a trademark race: she was fourth at the first turn, then sixth and still sixth at halfway. But she didn't know where she was in the race. She was stuck with lane eight, and from there she couldn't see the leaders. All she could do was trust her stroke, trust her tempo and allow her stronger finish to kick in.

And that was when the crowd thing happened. Even in the water, in the middle of one of the races of her life, she could not blank out their noise. It sucked her along, she said: 'That's the difference of the home crowd, it brings you from eighth to seventh, it moves you on.'

Was there disappointment? Not a drop. As she paraded her medal proudly around the poolside, it was easy to sit and wonder at what she might do in the 800 metres freestyle. That is her event, where she is world champion and fastest in the world.
– Owen Slot

Opposite: The rain couldn't dampen Lizzie Armitstead's spirits as she won Team GB's first Olympic medal in the road race.
Left: Proud to the tips of her patriotic fingers, Rebecca Adlington took her place on the podium to receive her bronze medal.
Overleaf: Buckingham Palace and the Queen Victoria Memorial provided a thrilling backdrop, despite the rain, as the competitors (Lizzie Armitstead, right) raced to the finish line.

RUSSIA
29
29
8
DURA-ACE

Women's team
Artistic gymnastics

HOPES OF more medals were kept alive in the North Greenwich Arena as the gymnasts took to the bars. Expectations were high that the three-time world champion could win gold.

Beth Tweddle overcame a knee injury that she thought would leave her unable to walk into the arena, let alone compete, to produce the best score of the day on the uneven bars in the women's artistic gymnastics qualifying event.

Three months ago the world champion had keyhole surgery and is still sleeping with an ice machine strapped to her leg, but the 27-year-old produced a stunningly confident and complex performance to score 16.133. There were high hopes that she would cap her career with an Olympic title, but few anticipated that her team-mates would qualify for the team final.

It was astonishing that Rebecca Tunney, at 15 the youngest Briton at the Olympics, performed without any sign of nerves. Tunney, nicknamed Twiglet by her team-mates, qualified for the all-around final, scoring 56.391 from the four pieces of apparatus – bars, beam, floor and vault.

Tweddle calmed her nerves with a quirky floor display. She chose 'Live and Let Die' by Paul McCartney & Wings; she said he had asked, via his PA, when she would be competing, so she hoped he had watched the event.

– Alyson Rudd

Hannah Whelan and Beth Tweddle share an emotional moment after qualifying for the Olympic final.

David Florence

Canoe slalom

OUTSIDE THE roaring descent of the Lee Valley White Water Centre's Olympic course, there is the flat calm of the River Lee with families rambling along its towpath. Echoing the water's mixed emotions, British canoeists and kayakers battled nerves and rapids in their quest for gold.

They sat atop the tall grandstands and cheered and waved their flags even if they did not know a canoe from a gnu or a Slovak champion from a no-hoper from nowhere in particular.

The 12,000 spectators in the Lee Valley White Water Centre's Olympic course filled the air with cheers, even when there was more turbulent water in the grandstands than there was on the stunning slalom course as a storm swept in with only a few minutes left of the first day of Olympic competition in the men's singles canoe and kayak categories.

'I have never heard anything like it,' David Florence, one of Britain's medal hopes, said after qualifying for the semi-finals of the C1 canoeing. 'It was simply fantastic.'

Florence left it very late to make qualification. He was a lowly thirteenth on his first run down the tumbling 300-metre course, which was not quite where the new world No 1 expected to be. That meant a session of heart-searching, video studying and course walking before he embarked on his second attempt.

But there was inspiration in those grandstands, a roar at the start that the man from Aberdeen, a silver medal-winner in Beijing in 2008, had not experienced before. He was the last of the 17 competitors to attempt to beat the clock.

One minute and 33 seconds later it was all over; Florence was safe and can now attempt to add Olympic gold to his status as the world's top C1 paddler.

– Kevin Eason

Zara Phillips

Equestrianism

ON A DAY when the thunder and lightning that played round Greenwich Park was almost as dramatic as the action in the arena, Britain's three-day-event team, helped by superb performances from Kristina Cook on Miners Frolic, Zara Phillips on High Kingdom and William Fox-Pitt on Lionheart, moved into the bronze-medal position.

With fewer than eight points separating the three teams there is everything to play for in the cross country which, with its steep gradients and twisting course, is expected to be the most influential phase.

Phillips, going early in the day and watched by her grandfather, the Duke of Edinburgh, and her mother, the Princess Royal, produced a solid performance on High Kingdom that left her in joint 24th place. Phillips said, 'I was really pleased with him [High Kingdom]. At Burghley he was a bit spooky but he coped really well today.'

The pecking order could change dramatically when the 74 riders face Sue Benson's 28-fence cross-country course over the steepest and most twisty terrain most of the riders will ever have encountered. All the riders have had to walk the course a minimum of four times to try to work out their line. 'They are not huge fences,' Mary King said. 'But the speed required will cause the mistakes.' She should have no problem with the steepness as she trains Imperial Cavalier over the Devon hills, but he is a long-striding horse who will not be as adjustable as some.

Phillips, in contrast, has the advantage of High Kingdom's neat, pony stride but she does not underestimate the task ahead. 'It looks as if it will be really hard work', she said. 'There's no let-up, you've just got to keep riding.'

– Jenny MacArthur

‘The girls have done amazingly well. We have been working so hard together. Our combined bars routine was the best ever recorded by a Great Britain team.’
Beth Tweddle

Defying expectations, Team GB’s gymnastics squad put on an impressive performance to qualify for the artistic gymnastics final.

Day 3 Round Up

BOXING
Welterweight Fred Evans began his Olympic campaign with some swagger, with an 18–10 points win over Ilyas Abbadi, of Algeria. Next he faces Egidijus Kavaliauskas, a Lithuanian who stopped him in the quarter-finals at the World Championships.

BASKETBALL
Michelle Obama gave the United States powerful support, reserving a post-game hug for every player and coach after the overwhelming favourites scored a 98–71 win over France.

JUDO
Colin Oates produced the best win of his career but fell short of winning Great Britain's first judo medal in 12 years when he was beaten 2–0 by Cho Jun Ho, of South Korea, in the repechage in the under-66kg division.

VOLLEYBALL
The hopes of Great Britain's men marking their Olympic debut with a win at Earls Court were snuffed out by Bulgaria's brilliant defence as the Eastern European side cruised to a 3–0 victory. Great Britain were beaten 25–18, 25–20, 26–24.

SAILING
Iain Percy and Andrew Simpson, the defending Olympic Star champions, bounced back from eleventh place in their first race to all but dead-heat with Robert Scheidt and Bruno Prada, the world champions from Brazil, leaving the British pair fifth overall.

In the women's match racing, Kate and Lucy MacGregor had one race win and one loss on their Olympic debut.

SHOOTING
Kimberly Rhode made history as the first American to win individual medals at five successive Games. The 33-year-old also equalled the world record with 99 hits out of 100 in the women's skeet.

TABLE TENNIS
Joanna Parker battled bravely but was eliminated from the women's singles in the second round when Kristin Silbereisen claimed a 4–1 victory. In the men's event, Paul Drinkhall upset the odds to beat Yang Zi 4–1.

MEDAL TABLE

				T
1. CHINA	6	4	2	12
2. USA	3	5	3	11
3. ITALY	2	3	2	7
4. SOUTH KOREA	2	1	2	5
5. FRANCE	2	1	1	4
16. GREAT BRITAIN	0	1	1	2

TOP NATIONS: SWIMMING MEDALS IN NUMBERS

USA

12

(4G 5S 3B)

FRANCE

3

(3G 0S 0B)

CHINA

5

(2G 2S 1B)

30.07.12
London 2012 Olympic Games
Day 4

Medals won by Team GB
Gold 0
Silver 0
Bronze 1

4

Men's team
Gymnastics

THE DISAPPOINTMENT of a day short on medals disappeared as five British gymnasts mounted a podium with their unbeatable Asian counterparts. Their bronze medal-winning performance was celebrated as raucously as any home success at these Games.

Forget the downgrading controversy in which Britain believed for 15 minutes that they had won silver – Louis Smith, Sam Oldham, Max Whitlock, Daniel Purvis and Kristian Thomas did not give it a second's thought.

They were too busy rejoicing in a performance of extraordinary skill and nerve, in which 17 of their 18 routines went as well as they could have dared to hope.

'A beautiful day for the sport,' Smith said. Not to mention loud, nail-biting, terrifying and, ultimately, glorious. Smith had got it off to a promising start when he scored 15.966 on his specialist apparatus, the pommel horse, sparking the first crowd eruption of the evening. With routines taking place simultaneously, there was action in every corner.

If this was about excelling, it also required the five-man team (three chosen for each of the six pieces of apparatus) to avoid calamity. And Team GB could breathe a little easier when they moved off from the rings, the weakest of their rotations. Confidence was growing and it soared when Thomas landed the best vault of the night – and the best of his life. His 16.550 was the biggest single score of the entire evening, a vault that sent him somersaulting up to the roof until he landed on two solid feet with perfection.

Team GB faced the last discipline in fourth place, behind Ukraine, knowing that they had to finish in style. They moved on to the mat and, with Ukraine already finished on the rings, Thomas knew that a medal was within his reach. That was quite something to consider as he held his handstand, but this was another brilliant performance from Thomas, who came off to be high-fived by Purvis, the brilliantly consistent all-rounder who was the only British gymnast to complete all six disciplines.

The crowd cheered what they assumed would be a bronze. Then came those 15 minutes of confusion after Kohei Uchimura's poor score in the final pommel routine was the subject of an inquiry. The Japanese, shell-shocked when second turned to fourth in one bad landing, protested at his score and were returned to the silver-medal position.

Bronze to silver then back to bronze, but Britain were delighted either way on an historic evening.
– Matt Dickinson

Left: The team relish their moment taking bronze on the podium
Below: Smith got the team off to a great start with an impressive score on the pommel horse
Opposite: Purvis, the only gymnast to compete in all six disciplines, put in a brilliant performance on the rings.

London 2012
London 2012

Tom Daley and Peter Waterfield

Synchronised diving

THE CHEERS of support reached the diving boards and beyond, but they couldn't bring Tom Daley and Peter Waterfield into a medal-winning position.

It was the fourth dive that did it. They had started so strongly in the Olympic 10-metres pairs final: three rounds out of six completed and the scoreboard showed the pair leading Cao Yuan and Zhang Yanquan, of China. The fourth dive went horribly wrong from the moment they leapt from the platform.

Waterfield said: 'On the fourth dive I had a great start, spinning really well, and just kicked my feet a bit too high and that meant I over-rotated.'

Daley refused to lay blame, saying: 'We win together, we lose together. We did the best we had today. The crowd have been amazing, It was all we dreamt of and to come fourth was so agonising.'

China claimed gold again, with Cao and Zhang notching up a dominant 486.78 points. Germán Sánchez Sánchez and Iván García Navarro, of Mexico, won the silver medal with 468.90 and Nicholas McCrory and David Boudia, of the United States, on 463.47, took bronze.

Daley said: 'Being so close is tough when you see other people standing on the podium, but that's sport and it's going to give us more motivation going into the individual event. You have to think you will win a medal and believe in yourself.'

– Craig Lord

Zoe Smith

Weightlifting

THE GLORY of the Olympics isn't just about winning medals, but also doing your best against the greatest athletes in the world and perhaps even setting a new record.

This was the story for 18-year-old Zoe Smith, who broke an eight-year British record in the clean and jerk and, in the process, exposed weightlifting to a new audience.

By lifting 121kg – or more than twice her body weight – Smith dispelled a host of preconceptions about a sport that had never been cheered by so many in a British venue. Few could not be charmed by her after she revealed she felt that she had let everyone down in the snatch event, where she lifted 90kg on her first attempt, but recorded two no-lifts with her second and third attempts at 93kg.

The roar of the home crowd lifted the rafters as she came out confidently to start at 116kg. On her second attempt, at 121kg, her legs wobbled and it was a no-lift, but she pulled it off at the third go and the crowd went wild.

On paper, for an hour at least, Smith was in the silver-medal position. But with stronger, more experienced women to follow in group A, in the end Smith finished twelfth as Li Xueying, of China, won gold with a lift of 138kg in the clean and jerk, for an overall total of 246kg. Pimsiri Sirikaew, of Thailand, picked up silver, while Yuliya Kalina, from Ukraine, captured bronze.

– Ashling O'Connor

Below left: Tom Daley and Peter Waterfield started well in the 10-metre pairs.
Below: Teenager Zoe Smith lifted her sport to new heights in the women's weightlifting.

Below: A moment of reflection for Gemma Spofforth after she just missed out on a medal in the 100 metres backstroke.

Bottom: Team-mate Liam Tancock also had to settle for fifth place after a determined performance in his 100 metres backstroke heat.

Gemma Spofforth

100 metres backstroke

FOR GEMMA Spofforth, there was no disappointment at missing out on a medal; for her, the glory of the Olympics will be remembering her journey to the Games.

Spofforth's story does not finish with a place on the podium in the 100 metres backstroke, it does not have quite that stunning wham-bam would-you-believe-it ending. It ended instead in lane seven, agonisingly close. Fifth.

It was special to see her walk out on to the pooldeck, introduced by the MC in the Aquatics Centre, her name chanted by the crowd. There have been times when this never seemed likely. Really not remotely.

Swimming and the Olympics seem small beer set against all her frighteningly painful personal history: the death of her mother, Lesley, from cancer in 2007, the death four years later of her father's girlfriend, June, and then June's daughter Vicky, both of them to cancer too.

She did not care much for swimming; she did not care much for anything. Some time between then and the Olympics, she found the love for her sport that she had so completely lost.

'I really wanted a medal,' she said. Indeed, she was in the fight right to the last ten metres, but she could not quite stay with Missy Franklin of the United States, or Emily Seebohm, of Australia, or Aya Terakawa, of Japan, who took bronze. But, she said: 'For me, it's rekindling that love and finding something I'm really passionate about and having fun with life again. That is what I'm going to take from this meet.'

She was not the only Briton to finish here. Liam Tancock came fifth in the 100 metres backstroke. The gold medal went to Matthew Grevers, of the United States. After the biggest race of his life, Tancock did not appear to regret his failure at winning a medal, instead saying that 'things are going well'. Well? 'I'm pleased,' he explained. 'It's progressing in the right direction.'

Another British finalist, Robbie Renwick, finished sixth in the 200 metres freestyle, though his triumph was simply getting to that final. There were other impressive performances from Caitlin McClatchey in the 200 metres freestyle and Hannah Miley in the 200 metres individual medley. Both reached the finals.

– *Owen Slot*

Liam Tancock watches the United States celebrate gold after a hard-fought race in which he came fifth.

Day 4 Round Up

TABLE TENNIS
Paul Drinkhall, the British No 1, fell in the third round in the men's singles against Dimitrij Ovtcharov, of Germany. Drinkhall had caused a small upset in his previous match, defeating Yang Zi, of Singapore, but Ovtcharov, the world No 12, beat him in four straight games.

SAILING
After finishing sixth and twelfth in the two races on the second day of the Finn class regatta off Weymouth, Ben Ainslie fell from second to third, 11 points behind the leader, Jonas Hogh-Christensen of Denmark.

In the Star class, Iain Percy and Andrew Simpson, the gold medal-winners in Beijing, are top after four races. Robert Scheidt and Bruno Prada, the world champions from Brazil, dropped from first to fourth.

HOCKEY
Barry Middleton led the way for Great Britain, scoring a goal in each half as they opened their campaign with an emphatic 4–1 victory over Argentina.

Elsewhere in the group, the pre-tournament favourites and world champions, Australia, cruised past South Africa 6–0 after leading 2–0 at the break, and Spain cancelled out Pakistan's 46th-minute goal within a minute to finish in a 1–1 draw.

FENCING
Shin A Lam, of South Korea, staged a teary 75-minute sit-down protest after her dreams of Olympic gold were shattered by a controversial ruling.

She sat on the piste in floods of tears after losing her semi-final in the women's epee to Britta Heidemann, of Germany, in the final second of a sudden-death extra minute.

BOXING
On a day characterised by complaints and appeals, Sumit Sangwan, the Indian boxer, has his appeal against a judges' decision turned down. Ajay Maken, the Indian Sports Minister, lodged an official protest after Yamaguchi Florentino, of Brazil, won the 81kg contest 15–14.

MEDAL TABLE

	Gold	Silver	Bronze	T
1. CHINA	9	5	3	17
2. USA	5	7	5	17
3. FRANCE	3	1	3	7
4. NORTH KOREA	3	0	1	4
5. ITALY	2	4	2	8
20. GREAT BRITAIN	0	1	2	3

GYMNASTICS: MEN'S TEAM FINAL

Gold CHN

275.997

Silver JAP

271.952

Bronze GBR

271.711

31.07.12
London 2012 Olympic Games
Day 5

Medals won by Team GB
Gold 0
Silver 1
Bronze 0

5

Equestrian team
Eventing

DAY 5 PROVED that Team GB is taking seriously the Olympic values of respect, excellence and friendship. None more so than the equestrian team when their gold medal hopes were dashed after Zara Phillips' showjumping round. The team shrugged off disappointment, closed ranks and dismissed the suggestion that any one team member was responsible for the step down on the podium.

However, this was the scene at the end of the eventing team competition, when Britain had won silver. Andrew Hoy, the Australian rider, approached Phillips to congratulate her: 'I said: "Congratulations, it's a great result." And she said: "I find it hard to feel that at the moment when I had the faults that I did."'

The bare facts are: Britain finished second behind Germany by 4½ points and in Phillips's showjumping round, her mistakes cost the team seven. That is not an apportioning of blame, it is a statement of fact.

At the start of the day, Britain were lying in second place. The riders knew that they needed clear rounds to challenge for gold. Phillips, riding High Kingdom, cleared the first fence and then hit the second. That was four penalty points immediately. Thereafter, she managed to recover well and she was clear. However, she was not fast enough and incurred a further three penalties.

The leading riders, Mary King and Kristina Cook, were yet to ride. King rode clear and punched the air as she departed the arena. Cook was nigh on perfect, too; she was clear but incurred a single penalty for being a second too slow.

The damage was done. However, this was a joyful occasion and an historic one. Phillips became the first British royal to win an Olympic medal; the medal ceremony was inevitably one of the moments of the Games.

When the five riders from the three teams trotted to the podium, a smile spread across the face of the Princess Royal as she stepped out to present the medals. New Zealand, who finished third, were presented with their medals first, then Britain, with Phillips in the middle. After giving medals to William Fox-Pitt and Nicola Wilson, the Princess Royal hung the silver medal round her daughter's neck and then completely broke with decorum by kissing her on both cheeks. Emotional times indeed.

– Owen Slot

Left: Mary King was delighted to ride a clear round in the showjumping event and help her team-mates on to a silver medal. **Opposite:** Beth Tweddle and her team-mates have proved that British gymnastics has an impressive future at the Olympic Games.

Women's team
Football

ON AN UPLIFTING, record-breaking night the women's football team secured first place in group E and underlined their status as genuine medal contenders.

Stephanie Houghton scored the only goal as early as the second minute, but, as compelling as the full-back's story as the goalscoring revelation of this tournament might be, this was a night that transcended individual glory.

'It was fantastic,' Powell said. 'I have never experienced that before. Usually when I shout on the touchline, the girls can hear me. Tonight was a good excuse for them to ignore me.' Powell's players followed her instructions to the letter. It was possible to pick out individuals in addition to Houghton but their new admirers will have been impressed by the work of the collective.

Britain held firm and at the end the players celebrated as enthusiastically as the fans.
– *Oliver Kay*

Women's team
Gymnastics

IN THE NORTH Greenwich Arena, another British team refused to be disappointed at their result.After all, this was not a blip in the stunning story of British gymnastics. After the men's remarkable success in the team event, all things felt possible and a sixth-place finish from Beth Tweddle and her team-mates, provided proof enough that women's artistic gymnastics is blossoming after Britain posted their best postwar result in the team competition.

'We've finished sixth. Four years ago we didn't even make the team final. The belief within the camp, Lottery funding, our coaches, the medical support, everyone that's helped us today, are the ones we've got to thank,' said Tweddle.

All five women were determined to use the success of the men's team as inspiration. 'We were never going to go out to try and replicate them,' Hannah Whelan said. 'We're really happy for them and we've done the best we could do.'
– *Alyson Rudd*

Michael Phelps

Men's 4 x 200 metres freestyle

MICHAEL PHELPS may have thought that he was ending a debate when he stood on a podium with his nineteenth Olympic medal (and his fifteenth gold), a haul that will surely not be matched until a human baby pops out with fins for feet.

But as Phelps made history, he may also have ignited a million pub arguments about whether having the most medals is the same thing as Greatest Olympian of All Time (GOAT).

Yet this is the sort of argument that will never bring closure. On a podium all of his own above Carl Lewis, who won the long jump at four consecutive Games, along with five sprint golds? Beyond the reach of Steve Redgrave and Emile Zatopek? And what of Larisa Latynina, the gymnast whose tally of 18 medals (nine gold) Phelps passed?

In a night that did not, it must be said, lack emotion, first came the shock of seeing Phelps draw level with Latynina on 18 medals while providing more evidence of his waning powers. In the 200 metres butterfly, his strongest event, he was beaten to the touch by Chad Le Clos when gold seemed his. But then came that final relay leg. His US team-mates had given him a huge lead and Phelps could savour the moment.

The very haul of medals that makes Phelps a phenomenon is held against him. The more

he amasses, the more people carp about gongs coming easy for the swimmers. Give Usain Bolt a 50-metre dash, a backwards sprint and a three-legged relay and he would be on 18 too, goes the argument.

But if it is reasonable to say that the sheer tally of medals should not automatically grant Phelps the garlands for GOAT, it seems extraordinarily graceless to hold the sport's array of disciplines against unarguably the greatest swimmer the world has seen.

True, the Phelps we are watching in London is, at 27, a fading force. He may leave the capital without a single individual title. He has three events left and the younger breed such as Le Clos and Ryan Lochte are coming past fast.

But we cannot forget that Phelps has redefined the parameters of his sport, with his eight historic golds in Beijing, his 39 world records, his 26 world titles and now a haul of Olympic medals that is not yet completed. So while these Games may show a great American sporting hero in decline, we should perhaps marvel more that he is putting up a fight.

Phelps has struggled to find motivation since Beijing, at times to the immense frustration of Bob Bowman, the coach and brains behind the operation. For years he clung to the memory of the teacher who told a kid with attention deficit disorder that he would 'never achieve anything in life'. But who is there to prove wrong when you are already the greatest swimmer of all time?

These Games are showing a vulnerable champion, but Phelps is a champion nevertheless with a fifteenth gold round his neck. That alone may not end the argument – but Phelps and his 19 medals is where you have to start.
– *Matt Dickinson*

After taking silver in the 200 metres butterfly, Michael Phelps went on to win gold with his US team-mates in the 4 x 200 metres freestyle and also set a new world record.

A group hug in the Aquatics Centre, as Michael Phelps celebrated a victorious 4 x 200m freestyle relay with his team-mates, and headed into retirement as the most decorated Olympian of all time

Day 5 Round Up

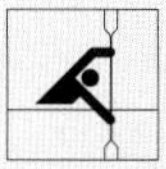

CANOEING

David Florence's medal hopes ended in the C1 canoe slalom as he was eliminated in the semi-final. The 29-year-old Scot won a silver medal in Beijing four years ago and entered the competition as world No 1, but as the eighth starter in the 12-strong field, with eight making it through to the final, he came only tenth.

Tony Estanguet, 34, of France, claimed his third Olympic title in the event, having won gold in Sydney in 2000 and Athens four years later. Sideris Tasiadis, of Germany, won silver, and Michal Martikan, of Slovakia, the gold medal-winner in 1996 and 2008, the bronze.

FENCING

In the men's foil competition British fencers James-Andrew Davis, Richard Kruse and Husayn Rosowsky were eliminated in their first matches at the ExCel Centre.

JUDO

Gemma Howell suffered a controversial defeat in the women's Olympic individual judo competition. Howell was disqualified from her bout with Gevrise Emane, of France, for a leg grab. Euan Burton lost to a young Canadian, Antoine Valois-Fortier, making his Olympic debut.

SAILING

With a solid fourth and third, Ben Ainslie pulled himself up to second place in the Finn class, but Jonas Hoegh-Jensen has a ten-point lead.

Star fleet leaders Iain Percy and Andrew Simpson also passed their midway point, on course to become the first crew to defend the men's Star Olympic title.

DIVING

Tonia Couch and Sarah Barrow, Great Britain's representatives in the women's synchronised ten-metre platform event, missed out on an Olympic medal as the Chinese once again proved the dominant force. The highly competitive final was won by Chen Ruolin and Wang Hao, of China.

The Britons were second after the compulsory dives, but dropped to sixth after Barrow over-rotated on the pair's third dive, before recovering to finish fifth.

BASKETBALL

Great Britain squandered a late chance to claim a big scalp in the men's tournament, losing 67–62 to Brazil.

MEDAL TABLE

				T
1. CHINA	13	6	4	23
2. USA	9	8	6	23
3. FRANCE	4	3	4	11
4. SOUTH KOREA	3	2	3	8
5. NORTH KOREA	3	0	1	4
11. GREAT BRITAIN	0	2	2	4

IN NUMBERS

World records	Total world records so far
0	**6**

Olympic records	Total Olympic records so far
4	**24**

WiGG

01.08.12
London 2012 Olympic Games
Day 6

Medals won by Team GB
Gold 2
Silver 1
Bronze 2

6

Heather Stanning and Helen Glover

Women's pairs

IT IS HARD to know what 'thoroughly British' means – but standing by a rowing lake near Windsor on Day 6 was to be sure of how it feels.

Thousands of Union Jacks were waving, a crowd were screaming themselves hoarse and two smashing women were about to win the first British gold of London 2012 to burst an emotional dam. Pent-up anxieties were unleashed in a rush of relief, joy and national pride. Heather Stanning and Helen Glover, the first British women ever to win Olympic gold in rowing, had done so with exquisite timing.

They crushed their opponents. And, if it looked ridiculously easy to you sitting on a sofa, remember that no one wins Olympic gold in rowing without intense suffering.

Stanning is a captain in the Royal Artillery who could be on active service next month in Afghanistan. Behind Stanning in Britain's golden boat was Glover, the trainee PE teacher who turned herself from a novice rower into an Olympic gold medal-winner inside four years.

These are two women you underestimate at your peril. As British rowing almost did a couple of years back. They were spares, without a crew to row in. They were thrown together by chance. Glover was still a raw product of the Talent ID project who watched the Beijing Games certain she was out of her depth. At the same time, Stanning was being commissioned at Sandhurst.

The pair were ahead from the first stroke. Victory was assured before halfway, though it still felt nerve-racking as the Australians and Kiwis closed the gap. Glover wept with joy, Stanning waved and a nation erupted with delight.

– *Matt Dickinson*

Men's rowing

Men's Eights

AND THAT WASN'T the end of the drama at Eton Dorney. A few hours later, veteran Olympic rower Greg Searle and his team-mates added another medal to GB's haul. Choking back emotion, the disappointment of Constantine Louloudis at bronze was clear, but so was the ambition of his crew and what they had done to try to achieve it.

'If we had wanted a silver medal, we would have got a silver medal,' the 20-year-old stroke said on his return to the Eton College lake where he had learnt to row. 'We went for the win, we went for gold and in our last 250 [metres] my legs had nothing left. I had given everything and was hoping the other seven had enough to carry me over.' Doubtless the seven others had the same thought. This was a tough, brutal, fabulous race. Germany, unbeaten this Olympiad, had made their customary fast start but Britain clung to them all the way down Dorney Lake, never letting them pull more than a seat in front.

A little after halfway Britain made their move, digging deep, rowing hard and putting every ounce of their being into each stroke. They carved, they splashed, they drove and gradually they moved past Germany. If not the whole seat's advantage that Phelan Hill, the cox, had shouted to them as encouragement, certainly they had their bow well in front. But Germany had another gear, pushed back and that was the battle over. Having given everything to break them, Britain had almost broken themselves. In the final 500 metres they were passed by a sprinting Canada and almost by the United States. To lose a bronze medal after that effort would have been cruel.
– *Patrick Kidd*

In a tough, brutal race the men's eights gave it their all. They missed out on gold but came home with a well-deserved bronze.

Bradley Wiggins and Chris Froome

Men's time trial

At the historic royal palace at Hampton Court, meanwhile, an Olympic legend was making history by winning his seventh medal.

Standing in the sun, receiving a medal in front of the palace, was like the last splash of colour in a work of art. Bradley Wiggins's victory had the leafy streets of Surrey howling with pleasure, but it was just the finishing touch in what has been arguably the greatest year by any road cyclist in history.

Wiggins is piling up outstanding achievements: never before had a Tour de France winner gone on to win gold in the same year; Sir Steve Redgrave had seemed the ultimate British Olympian with six Olympic medals, but Wiggins has seven; never before had a British sportsman led so many denizens of the home counties into standing on the side of the road with huge red sideburns painted on their faces.

They came out to watch him in the Olympic time trial, a 44-kilometre race-against-the-clock on a loop from Hampton Court, down to Cobham in Surrey, up the Thames and back. Wiggins was the penultimate rider on the course and as he swept through the Surrey streets it became increasingly clear that he was the fastest.

Tony Martin of Germany was his closest rival but the cheers of Wiggins's followers as he returned to Hampton Court told the story. He finished ahead of Martin by 42 seconds. His unbeaten record in time trials this year was intact.

His season has been a masterpiece and the Olympic time trial was the final touch. For most of it he had by his side an able lieutenant. Chris Froome, 27, born in Kenya to a British father, has also pulled off one of the most successful seasons by any British cyclist. Wiggins's success in the Tour de France was assisted by his team-mate. Yet, for all his sacrifice, Froome still came second. And to add to Wiggins's gold medal, Froome contributed a bronze.

– Owen Slot

Wiggins pushes for gold with the cheers of the home crowd behind him.

50m
100m

Michael Jamieson

200 metres breaststroke

Jamieson broke a Commonwealth record on his way to giving himself an early birthday present – a silver Olympic medal.

AS NIGHT FELL over the Olympic Park and Day 6 began to draw to a close, Michael Jamieson celebrated his 24th birthday four days early with a silver medal – and he was only 0.15 seconds away from the ultimate two prizes won by Daniel Gyurta, the 200 metres breaststroke world champion from Hungary: Olympic gold in a world-record time of 2 minutes 7.28 seconds.

Posting 2:07.43 – a Commonwealth record and the second-best under the present suit rules – Jamieson, the first Briton to win a breaststroke medal in 20 years, kept alive a British tradition with a surge of speed in the home straight at the Aquatics Centre, the wave of sound bouncing off the rafters sweeping him to silver.

If only the pool had been a hand longer. Jamieson, a Glaswegian who chose swimming over football at 13 because it was warmer in the pool in winter, was the only man in the race who swam the last of the four lengths inside 33 seconds, his 32.62 surge for the wall precisely half a second swifter than Gyurta's last lap to take gold.

The gap to Gyurta was reduced with every burning stroke in the last 20 metres of the race, but the world champion, who has been on a passionate hunt for Olympic gold, refused to yield. Finding a reserve of energy to hold off the British assault, Gyurta reached the wall first in the nick of time, Jamieson a stroke shy of causing a big upset, Ryo Tateishi denying his team-mate by 0.06 seconds in 2:08.29 as Andrew Willis faded to last in 2:09.44.
– Craig Lord

Day 6 Round Up

GYMNASTICS
Kohei Uchimura of Japan ended his wait for Olympic gold in the men's all-round gymnastics final. Marcel Nguyen took silver, Danell Leyva bronze.

BADMINTON
Eight badminton players – from China, South Korea and Indonesia – were disqualified for trying to lose their final group matches in order to secure an easier quarter-final draw.

CANOEING
Despite deafening support, Richard Hounslow, 30, Britain's top slalom kayaker, was twelfth out of 15 in the men's kayak singles K1 semi-final at the Lee Valley White Water Centre, two short of a place in the final, won by Daniele Molmenti, of Italy.

JUDO
Winston Gordon, 35, gave Britain's judo team a much-needed boost as he beat Alexandre Émond, of Canada, with an ippon, although he lost his second contest in the under-90kg division, to Kirill Denisov, of Russia.

Sally Conway, 25, also won her first contest, against Carine Ngarlemdana, of Chad, but then lost to Edith Bosch, of the Netherlands, the eventual bronze medal-winner.

The gold in the men's under-90kg division went to Song Dae Nam, of South Korea, while the women's under-70kg gold was won by Lucie Décosse, of France.

SAILING
Lighter than forecast wind conditions helped Paul Goodison complete his two opening races and reach his first rest day. After securing a fourth and ninth place, he is now in sixth.

Nick Dempsey, the 2004 bronze medal-winner, put a shaky start behind him with a race win that promoted him to third in the RS:X windsurfer fleet.

In the 49er class, Stevie Morrison and Ben Rhodes scored second and fourth places and are within ten points of second overall, with ten races to sail.

BASKETBALL
A 67–61 defeat by Russia makes it extremely difficult for Great Britain's women basketball team to qualify for the quarter-finals.

MEDAL TABLE

				T
1. CHINA	17	9	4	30
2. USA	12	8	9	29
3. SOUTH KOREA	6	2	4	12
4. FRANCE	5	3	5	13
5. NORTH KOREA	4	0	1	5
11. GREAT BRITAIN	2	3	4	9

ROWING: WOMEN'S PAIRS FINAL

Gold GBR

7:27.13

Silver AUS

7:29.86

Bronze NZ

7:30.19

GREAT

02.08.12
London 2012 Olympic Games
Day 7

Medals won by Team GB
Gold 3
Silver 3
Bronze 0

7

Men's cycling team
Track sprint

FOR FOUR years we have been waiting for what would unfold here in this beautiful Olympic Velodrome, the hall of dreams with the wavy roof they nicknamed the Pringle. We wondered if Sir Chris Hoy, the giant of the Beijing Games, had a repeat performance in him, if 36 years of age was too much to recreate all that glory.

Hoy may have been the headline and the star performer, but as he generously said afterwards, it was not he who made the crucial difference here, driving the team under two world records to gold, it was the other two on the podium next to him – Jason Kenny and Philip Hindes.

Yet two years ago, Hoy would barely have heard of Hindes. Only if he paid close attention to the results of world junior events might he have done, but those results did not indicate the potential that had yet to be unleashed, nor did they tell him that this young German boy was born to a British father and was itching to switch sides. For the London Olympics, Hoy and Kenny could find no launch pad, no Man One – as they are known – to ride the first lap and then fire them down the track to glory.

So there we were, a packed Pringle – stomachs twisted with tension – wondering if this 19-year-old they had opted for could possibly be the missing ingredient.

He hardly soothed nerves in the qualifying round when he rolled off the start gate 20 yards round the track and then fell off his bike. The extraordinary rules of this event allowed them to reload and start again, but you could only wonder how he would cope.

The speed of the track and the quality of this field were clear from the very start of the competition. First the Chinese broke the Olympic record, then the Russians lowered it, then the French took it even lower. Last in qualifying were Britain.

We knew the game. There were two exceptionally fast teams here: Britain and France. In the first round France were so good they went under the Olympic record again. Britain took a look at that and went even better – they beat the world record. They had sniffed this record in training. As Hoy said: 'We knew it was possible, but knowing it and delivering it are two different things.'

The improvement had to come from Hindes. Only two weeks ago, in training, Hindes was still doing 17.6. However, he was confident that in the electric atmosphere he could bring that down nearer 17.3. When they broke that record in the first round, Hindes's lap was 17.265. He had surpassed the hopes of himself and everyone else.

The final, then, brought the French to the line again, but now the Britain trio were purring. Hindes delivered again – 17.274. Then Kenny took over and, as Hoy said, 'His lap was phenomenal, I was hanging in there.' It just required Hoy to finish it off. And he did so with another world record.

'When I crossed the line and heard the roar,' he said, 'I knew I'd won the race. When you step in the Velodrome and feel the atmosphere,' he said, 'it's like nothing else. It's not easy to put into words how happy I am.'

– *Owen Slot*

Chris Hoy celebrates beating France to the gold medal after an impressive team performance in the men's team sprint.

Peter Wilson
Men's double trap

ANOTHER WORLD RECORD holder had gold in his sights on Day 7. Two shots. Just two shots, the most important of Peter Wilson's young life, would seal gold at his home Olympic Games. As Wilson prepared to squeeze the trigger of his shotgun, his mind flashed across London to the Olympic Village and he wondered whether he would have time for a game of table tennis later.

If that sounds remarkably cool, Wilson admitted to a severe case of the shakes as he almost let slip a comfortable advantage in the final of the men's double trap shooting.

Finishing the job as fast as he could and avoiding the prospect of a tie that would mean shooting off with the seemingly nerveless Hakan Dahlby, who was stalking the world record-holder with astonishing determination, became the priority. Two final shots and it was over.

'I was thinking that if I can win this now, I am not going to have to faff around with any shoot-offs,' Wilson said with a chuckle of relief. 'That is the truth, that is what I was thinking. I wanted to get back and have a good game at the village. I am getting really into table tennis. It's sad, isn't it? I am pretty useless – in fact I am rubbish. I played a few athletes but I wouldn't dare name names because they all beat me. Desperately embarrassing.'

And slight embarrassment when Wilson sank to his knees at the Royal Artillery Barracks in Woolwich as he became champion. 'You think what you would do if you win Olympic gold and you don't really know until it happens,' Wilson said. 'But there has been a fair bit of build-up and a fair bit of ressure at our home games and when it comes together on the day it is an amazing experience, and one I will treasure for the rest of my life.'

– *Kevin Eason*

Peter Wilson kept his cool composure as he stared down the barrel of his gun, by thinking about playing ping-pong after his shooting final.

Etienne Stott and Tim Baillie

Canoe slalom

BACK ON the water at the Lee Valley, one of Team GB's two-man canoe slalom team had to overcome more than just the rapids if they were to have a fighting chance of reaching the podium.

When he was packing his kit for the final, Etienne Stott put his Great Britain medal-winner's tracksuit at the bottom of his bag. 'I left it in the plastic, I didn't think I'd need it,' he said.

Few would have disagreed with him, especially once he and Tim Baillie became the slowest of the six crews to qualify from the semi-final. In the final, not only would they be up against the British No 1 pairing, David Florence and Richard Hounslow, who were the fastest qualifiers, but also one of the greatest Olympic teams of recent times in the Hochschorner twins from Slovakia, Pavol and Peter, who had won this event at each of the previous three Games.

Baillie and Stott were the first to paddle their way down the 300 metres of violently churning water in the final, navigating their way through 23 gates along the way.

Baillie is the man kneeling at the front, generating momentum, while Stott acts as the rudder. When they completed the course without hitting any gates and recorded a faster time, 106.41 seconds, than any crew had managed in the semi-final, they knew that they had given it their all and were given a rapturous ovation by the crowd of 12,000 in the packed stands. 'We didn't know how good it was at that stage, but it was a good, honest effort,' Baillie said. 'We just had to sit and wait.'

Then the next three crews came down in slower times, meaning that they would be guaranteed a medal and that Stott would be needing that tracksuit. Then the Hochschorners came down and, struggling to arrest their canoe against the

'We didn't know how good it was at that stage, but it was a good, honest effort. We just had to sit and wait.' Tim Baillie

current, they hit a pole at gate 17 and incurred a two-second penalty. It was a costly mistake. Although they had descended quicker than the British pair, their time showed them 1.87 seconds behind.

So Great Britain were now assured of the gold, because Florence and Hounslow were the final crew to paddle. They too completed the course without penalties, but 0.36 seconds slower. The pair raised their paddles above their heads in triumph at their own silver medal, but also in the knowledge that a remarkable double had been achieved, including the first British gold in canoe slalom. Baillie and Stott leapt into the water and the four team-mates celebrated together. Shortly afterwards, Stott was able to rip the plastic off his tracksuit and dress to celebrate his success. The extrovert of the two, he jumped up and down on the podium and punched the air. There was no pomp in this very British medal ceremony.

Team-mates and rivals at the same time, there was an unmistakable warmth among the British quartet. Above all, there was a sense of pleasure that their backwater of a sport would have its day in the mainstream, a genuine Olympic story. – *John Westerby*

Men's rowing
Lightweight fours

AT ANOTHER bankside venue, Eton Dorney, a delighted home crowd saw Great Britain pick up a third medal from rowing, when the lightweight men's four were pipped into second place by South Africa in a sprint.

Having started the race poorly, down in fifth place after 500 metres, it was a fine achievement by Britain to drag themselves back into contention for the gold in what Richard Chambers, the No 3 man and Peter's elder brother, called 'a brutal race'.

As the boats passed the grandstands, it looked as if it would be between Britain, the best crew this season, and Denmark, the Olympic champions in Beijing. Australia, who had fought for the lead with the Danes for most of the race, were dropping back and would finish fourth.

Suddenly, on came South Africa, charging through the field led by their stroke, Sizwe Ndlovu, the first black African Olympic medal-winner in rowing. Ndlovu and his crew had the edge. They crossed the line almost bow-ball to bow-ball with Britain and Denmark, but a crucial quarter of a second ahead to take their country's first rowing gold. Britain snatched the silver medal from the Danes by only seven-hundredths of a second.

'The pain is extreme,' Chris Bartley, Britain's stroke, said. 'I don't remember much about the last 250 metres. I was sick quite a few times after the line.' For Rob Williams, in the No 2 seat, there was just exquisite relief at a medal and at having gained his PhD last month. 'The past two weeks could have gone very well or very badly for me,' he said.

There was a small hope that Britain would get a medal in the double sculls after Germany and Australia were knocked out in the semi-finals, but Sam Townsend and Bill Lucas, who led for the first 200 metres, slipped to fifth. The race was won by Nathan Cohen and Joseph Sullivan, the New Zealand pair.

It was never likely that Britain would win a medal in the women's eights and they clung to the rear until passing Australia in the final strokes to come fifth. The United States won by half a length from Canada, with the Netherlands third.
– Patrick Kidd

Below: Chris Bartley, Richard Chambers, Rob Williams and Peter Chambers thank the crowd for their applause at their silver-medal win.

Gemma Gibbons
Judo

THE MEDAL haul continued at the ExCel Centre as Gemma Gibbons astonished team-mates and supporters to become the first British Olympic judo medallist for 12 years.

It is little surprise Gibbons was in a daze. Wearing her Olympic silver medal, a welter of thoughts and emotions was going through her mind.

There had been tears, notably as she reached the final of the under-78kg competition with victory over Audrey Tcheuméo, the 2011 world and European champion from France. When she realised what she had done she looked to the skies and said, 'I love you, Mum', a message to her mother, Jeanette, who died from leukaemia in 2004.

There had been days of infighting in the sport, as the British squad seemed incapable of breaking their medal drought. But perhaps one of the biggest thrills was putting the smile back on the face of Euan Burton, her boyfriend. Two days ago, Burton had broken down in tears in front of the television cameras as his Olympic campaign came to a crashing halt in barely a minute.

Expectations had been high for Burton, but little was expected of Gibbons, who had moved up in weight only recently and held a world ranking of just 42. Yet she swept through the morning session, recording wins over Yahima Ramirez, of Portugal, and Purevjargalyn Lkhamdegd, of Mongolia, with dramatic late scores.

In the quarter-final, a last-minute wazuri secured victory over Marhinde Verkerk, of the Netherlands, to set up a semi-final against Tcheuméo, victory being secured by an ippon in the golden score extra period.

The final, against Kayla Harrison, of the United States, proved a step too far, as the American won with two minor yuko scores. But it was the first British Olympic medal in judo since the silver won by Kate Howey – now Gibbons's coach – in Sydney 12 years ago.

'As a kid growing up, she was my hero,' Gibbons said. 'The whole day is just a bit of a daze, but in the following days, weeks and months I will look back and think what a great moment that was.'
– *Ron Lewis*

Below: Gemma Gibbons (left) was a surprise finalist in the under-78kg judo competition, where she won silver after being overpowered by Kayla Harrison.

Women's cycling team
Track sprint

AFTER A spectacular day for British sport a cloud drifted over the Velodrome. Expectations were high for a medal from the women cyclists, but a split-second mistake dashed those hopes.

If it was a wretched night for the disqualified Victoria Pendleton and Jess Varnish, it was no better for the UCI, cycling's governing body. In a brilliant venue, on a magical night of sport, an Olympic event was reduced to farce.

What else can we conclude when the fastest team (China) are relegated to silver, the second quickest (Great Britain) go home tearfully with nothing and the Germans end up all but apologising for having gold medals around their necks?

Rules are rules, as Pendleton gracefully conceded in a round of interviews that began with her rueful smile and finished with her eyes turning a watery red and her lips trembling. 'We take responsibility,' she said.

It all comes down to a little bit of marker tape on the track to show the zone where the lead rider can pull up, with Varnish doing so too early and the Chinese just too late, though their infringement seemed fractional after numerous replays.

'Imagine if you drive a car at 65 kmph and there is a small white piece of tape on the road,' Kristina Vogel said. 'That is what you have to see (to mark the changeover).' In other words, damn difficult.

'We are talking like a hundredth of a second, a blink of an eye,' Pendleton said. 'Jess and I were going way faster than we've ever gone before. And it just happened so quickly. You are giving 100 per cent, thinking about every pedal rev. I am focusing on Jess's wheel, watching, watching, trying to time my change. It's not something that's easy to judge. It is difficult to tell where you are on the track when you are going as hard and fast as that.'

Pendleton said that they had practised the move thousands of times, but had made a fractional error as they hit new speeds in an arena built to break records. The British pair had set a world record in their first qualifying run, only to see it immediately beaten by the Chinese.

Above: Day 7 ended in disappointment for British hopes Victoria Pendleton and Jess Varnish in the Velodrome. **Opposite:** Before their disqualification, Pendleton and Varnish had set a new world record in their qualifying run.

But then came that fateful error when Varnish moved up just too early.

It cost Britain a certain silver medal, perhaps gold, though the Chinese had looked imperious. Boos rang out around the Velodrome after the announcement that the home duo would not be allowed to compete in the final.

As the British women accepted the hugs of sympathetic team-mates, Germany were promoted to take on China in the final.

There was no surprise when China won and Guo Shuang and Gong Jinjie embarked on a victory lap with coaches and officials. Then came the news that this race, too, was subject to an inquiry, which seemed to take forever with time for the crowd to conduct a Mexican wave in slow motion.

Fully 10 or 15 minutes later, to the fury of the Chinese pair, came the official verdict that they had been relegated to silver.

The Germans, meanwhile, found out from a BBC reporter in mid-interview that they were the new Olympic champions with a time of 32.798 seconds, far from the quickest of the night. Australia were awarded bronze.

– *Matt Dickinson*

Day 7 Round Up

ROWING
Britain won three semi-finals. Zac Purchase and Mark Hunter responded to an early challenge from France to win the lightweight men's double, while Kat Copeland and Sophie Hosking came from a canvas down with 500 metres remaining to win the women's version by three seconds from Greece.

HOCKEY
Great Britain swept to a third successive victory, beating Belgium 3–0. The win helped them to maintain top spot in the group, ahead of the Netherlands, the Olympic champions.

BASKETBALL
France chalked up an impressive 82–74 group victory against Lithuania.

HANDBALL
Great Britain's men lost to Argentina, their third successive defeat in the competition. They were outclassed in heavy losses to France, the Olympic and world champions, and Sweden, the three-times silver medal-winners, in their first two outings. However, their first-half display against the South Americans belied their infancy as a team.

BEACH VOLLEYBALL
Shauna Mullin and Zara Dampney qualified for a place in the next round as one of the four lucky losers put into the draw. This was despite the British team's defeat at the hands of Russia, who beat them 25–23, 21–13 in their last pool F match at Horse Guards Parade.

MEDAL TABLE

				T
1. CHINA	18	11	5	34
2. USA	18	9	10	37
3. SOUTH KOREA	7	2	5	14
4. FRANCE	6	4	6	16
5. GREAT BRITAIN	5	6	4	15

CYCLING: MEN'S TEAM SPRINT FINAL

Gold GBR

42.600

Silver FRA

43.013

adidas
adidas

03.08.12
London 2012 Olympic Games
Day 8

Medals won by Team GB
Gold 3
Silver 0
Bronze 4

8

Anna Watkins and Katherine Grainger

Women's double sculls

AFTER THE successes of Day 7, it was tempting to dream of a medal rush, but could Team GB do it two days in a row? They didn't have to wait long to find out; the day got off to a thundering start on the waters at Eton Dorney, as British rowing once again brought home the gold.

It was an early-morning paddle in Cambridge a decade ago that changed the life of Anna Watkins and ultimately led to Great Britain winning their second rowing gold medal of the 2012 Olympics.

As the Newnham College first VIII trained on the Cam, their coach shouted through the megaphone. 'Looking good, Newnham,' he said. 'You'll give City Women a run for their money, except you, Anna.' The maths undergraduate from Leek, Staffordshire, looked up, concerned. 'You should be going to the Olympics,' he said.

She thought he was making fun of her, but the coach had identified something in the teenager. At the end of term, he made the same point to her.

She and Katherine came together in 2010 and have never lost, but it was the 23rd consecutive win that meant more than all the others.

Paul Thompson, the women's chief coach, knew that the gold medal would be won after 30 strokes. 'I could just see that it was going to be their day by the way they started,' he said. Watkins was less certain, publicly, at least, saying that she felt the race was won only when they got nearly a length clear of Australia shortly before the halfway mark. 'In the last 100 metres there was no way anyone could beat us,' she said. 'I felt very calm and had time to enjoy the race.'

– Patrick Kidd

Alan Campbell

Men's single sculls

THE EXCITEMENT at Eton Dorney did not end there. Not to be outdone by the women, the men's rowing team also had a point to prove.

Alan Campbell stood on the pontoon for the medals ceremony of the single sculls and wept copiously. It was not from frustration that he had won only the bronze medal, Great Britain's first in the event since 1928, nor through the pain still coursing through his limbs. He wept out of love for his parents, his friends and above all his wife, Jules. 'I don't think I have ever cried quite like that,' he said. 'It was pure emotion flooding out.'

From halfway in the final, it was a two-horse race for gold and silver, with Campbell scrapping with Lassi Karonen, of Sweden, for bronze. He admitted that the roar of the crowd had got him home first.

Campbell is the third rower from Coleraine, Northern Ireland, to win a medal this week, following the Chambers brothers in the lightweight four on Thursday. They had praised Campbell as their inspiration, but he said the small Northern Irish town is becoming a factory line for oarsmen. 'There's a lot of talent coming through,' he said. 'I can promise you that there will be better rowers than we are coming out of Coleraine.'

Another sign of Britain's future came in the final of the men's pair, where George Nash and Will Satch, in only their third regatta together, took a bronze medal behind the all-conquering New Zealanders, Hamish Bond and Eric Murray, and France. The Kiwis pulled away after 750 metres, finishing in 6 minutes 16 seconds, only eight seconds outside their world record.

'It has been an awesome year,' Satch said. 'I never knew this was going to happen six months ago. George has got such determination and we put everything into it.'

The Britain men's quad had achieved more than expected just by reaching their first Olympic final, but for half of it they clung to the side of Croatia, the favourites, as Germany forged ahead to the gold medal. The crew of Matt Wells, Steven Rowbotham, Charles Cousins and Tom Solesbury were unable to keep the momentum going in the third 500 metres, slipping to fifth by the finish.

– Patrick Kidd

adidas
TEAM GB
London 2012

Victoria Pendleton
Women's keirin

On Day 8, Victoria Pendleton returned to the Velodrome in fighting spirit to try to win the gold that had eluded her the previous day. With the home crowd willing her on, an Olympic medal before retirement seemed within reach.

When you are inside one of those space-age bike helmets, when the output in your legs is at the max, you do not hear. All that registers in terms of noise, explained Anna Meares, is the sound of your own breathing. But with a lap and a quarter to go of the keirin final, Meares finally heard the crowd. 'That,' she said, 'was when I could tell that she was coming'. 'She', of course, was Pendleton. And at that moment the volume also hit the max.

The swoop from behind was a move of fierce acceleration and a statement to her rivals: 'I am off, catch me if you can.' Behind her was Meares, the magnificent Australian against whom she came to London to do battle. Behind her, by 24 hours, was the disappointment of being disqualified in the team sprint event: that horrible spectre of failure. In front of her was the Olympic podium.

The disqualification on Thursday night might have hurt some athletes. Pendleton, however, came back fighting. The moment that Pendleton forged ahead, the five riders behind her, naturally, tried to follow. As they pelted down the back straight, the rivals lined up to take her. Guo Shuang, the Chinese former world champion, looked the most dangerous, Meares looked nowhere at all. Pendleton defended a shrinking lead, Shuang edging ever closer. But Pendleton held on; by less than half a wheel, it seemed that the Olympic obsession was finally worth it.

– Owen Slot

Men's cycling
Team pursuit

As the evening wore on, the cyclists added to Team GB's medal haul at the Velodrome in a sensational team effort.

Ed Clancy, Geraint Thomas, Steven Burke and Peter Kennaugh did more on Day 8 than merely beat the talented foursome of Jack Bobridge, Glenn O'Shea, Rohan Dennis and Michael Hepburn. In a final between two teams, Australia were fortunate to come second as the British quartet broke the world record for the second time in consecutive days, finishing in 3 minutes 51.659 seconds.

There had been a building of noise throughout the race and when they crossed the line, the sound was deafening. 'It was extraordinary,' Thomas said. 'I've never heard anything quite like that.'

Ed Clancy gave the British team such a strong start that they were almost half a second up halfway through the first lap. The Australians had dragged the deficit back to 0.31 seconds at the end of the first kilometre and, at the halfway point, the British lead was 0.56 seconds. At this point, the British quartet maintained their speed and the Australians started to crumble. At 3,000 metres, the gap between the teams was 1.47 seconds and, when the Australians crossed the line, it had grown to almost three seconds.

For Thomas and Clancy this was a second gold medal in the team pursuit. They set a world record winning gold in Beijing with Bradley Wiggins and Paul Manning. 'It's a special event, the team pursuit, and there's a bond between those lads that have ridden together,' Hunt said. Especially when you have beaten your fiercest rivals, broken the world record and won gold in the process.
– *John Westerby*

It all came together in the Velodrome for the gold medal-winning team of Clancy, Thomas, Burke and Kennaugh.

Rebecca Adlington
800 metres freestyle

WHILE BRITISH cycling continued to enjoy huge success, British swimming was still struggling to meet the medal tally expected of them at London 2012. The much-loved British swimmer Rebecca Adlington failed to defend her 800 metres freestyle title, but her valiant effort was rewarded with bronze.

As Rebecca Adlington's lips wobbled and her eyes reddened on the podium, a cry of 'Becky! Becky!' thundered around the Aquatics Centre.

There was sympathy because while Adlington's two bronze medals from the 400 metres and 800 metres were not all that she, or the crowd, had hoped for, they still represented high points for British swimming in these Olympics.

Adlington admitted that she was a couple of seconds outside expectations – though almost six behind Katie Ledecky – but the crowd were making another point: where would Britain have been without the fighter from Mansfield?

Adlington explained her struggle to cope as one of the poster girls of a home Games. 'The pressure, the expectations and everything going into this meet was difficult,' she said. 'I'm not going to lie, I'm not happy with that time. I've beaten it all year but everything seemed to catch up with me here.' Bronze in the shorter event was as much as Adlington had hoped for on form. But she, like the rest of us, was astonished as the script was transformed by Ledecky.

Adlington talked afterwards of feeling her age and how hard it was to recover these days from hard training sessions. If that sounded ridiculous from a 23-year-old, Ledecky's youth underlined the march of a new generation.

The duel we had expected to see was Adlington against her old rival Lotte Friis. The two quickest swimmers in the history of the event had also come into this 16-length showdown as the two fastest qualifiers. Adlington's best time of the year would have been enough for silver but she did not

Above: Despite being knocked into third place by the American sensation Katie Ledecky, Adlington described her home bronze as 'better than anything I've experienced in my entire life.'

Karina Bryant
Judo

have the strength to go with the teenager. With 200 metres remaining, Mireia Belmonte García, of Spain, attacked to finish second behind Ledecky's time of 8 minutes 14.63 seconds.

The youth of the new champion is something Adlington will have to weigh up as she considers whether to continue. 'I don't really know [about retirement],' she said. 'I still love the sport. I want to be normal for a little bit then sit down in October and see how much I have missed it. Some have said silver or bronze is losing, which to me is insane. Swimming is one of the hardest if not the hardest to medal at. I can happily say that I have been in four Olympic finals and medalled in all of them. I've beaten all my expectations. I didn't expect to be at the Olympics when I was little. I hope people are proud of me for getting that bronze.'

And, with that, there was another great cry of 'Becky! Becky!'
– *Matt Dickinson*

Above right: Karina Bryant is overcome with emotion at her bronze medal win against Iryna Kindzerska.

JUDO FANS have been treated with the sight of the rebirth of British hopes in their sport at London 2012. Only two days before, the future of British judo was being talked about in the gravest of terms. Two medals later and Great Britain can celebrate its best Olympic Games in the sport since 1992.

Karina Bryant's bronze medal in the women's heavyweight division, coming on the back of a silver medal for Gemma Gibbons in the women's under-78kg division, could not have been a better reply to those voices, some within the sport, who had been happy to give those in the national set-up a kicking when things had not gone too well.

Bryant, 33, a five-times collector of silver in the World Championships and a four-times gold medal-winner in the European Championships, had, in three previous Olympic Games, failed to get beyond the second round and was beaten in the first round in Beijing four years ago.

Bryant was never able to dominate her semi-final against Mika Sugimoto, of Japan. She did well in the grips, but twice came close to being swept. That led to her picking up two penalties that added up to a yuko and Sugimoto advanced to the final, giving Bryant a bronze-medal match against Iryna Kindzerska.

It proved to be a thriller. She took an early lead with a waza-ari, only for Kindzerska to level and edge ahead with a yuko. With one minute 42 seconds to go, Bryant pulled off a second waza-ari, which is equal to an ippon, and finished the match.

'We've had some disappointments in the team. Some will go away pretty gutted, but every single one of them fought their heart out. A couple of them got caught. That's judo. It's a tough sport. I believe every member of that team did the best they could,' said Bryant.
– *Ron Lewis*

Jessica Ennis
Heptathlon

Overleaf: Day one in the athletics stadium, and 80,000 spectators held their breath as Jessica Ennis competed in the shot put.
Below: Jessica Ennis put on a spectacular show for the home crowd, finishing the day tantalisingly close to securing her longed-for Olympic gold.

WHILE EVERYONE celebrated a rise up the medal rankings, in the stadium British athletes were setting up for a weekend that could push Team GB higher in the table.

When Jessica Ennis finished her first day of the Olympic heptathlon with a wind-beating personal best of 22.83 seconds in the 200 metres, it gave her a stunning first day score of 4,158 points.

She leads Austra Skujyte, of Lithuania, by 184 points and could win gold, break the British record and even breach the fabled 7,000-point barrier after a gilt-edged performance. She will probably knock up a Victoria sponge in the afternoon break such is her multitasking munificence.

The tide will have to turn in dramatic fashion, to wash away the foundations of all those goodies. Nobody should get too ahead of themselves, though, even if Ennis found herself getting far ahead of her main rivals, Tatyana Chernova, the world champion, and Nataliya Dobrynska, the Olympic champion. They were tenth and fourteenth respectively, a massive 309 and 323 points adrift.

As statements of intent go, the first event of the heptathlon was a tattoo on the forehead of Chernova and Dobrynska. Ennis ignored the crowd, forgot about the four years of toil, the broken ankle that ruined the last Olympic dream and ran a 100 metres hurdles that will remain etched into British sporting history. The time of 12.54 seconds came with manifold accolades. It was the fastest in a heptathlon. Only two specialist hurdlers had gone quicker this year.

Ennis backed up her crazy start with 1.86 metres in the high jump. Given that she is joint British record-holder in the event, that was par at best, but she was aided by her rivals buckling.

After the morning session and two of seven events, Ennis led Hyleas Fountain, of the United States, by 25 points. Katarina Johnson-Thompson, the 19-year-old from Liverpool, was in bronze medal place. Her limp shot put dropped her to twentieth, but it was a tantalising glimpse of the future.

– Rick Broadbent

Women's team
Football

While British supporters waited on tenterhooks to see what success the athletes could achieve in the rest of the Games, for the British women's football team Day 8 marked the end of their competition.

It was wonderful while it lasted, but the uplifting story of women's footballers at London 2012 ended in disappointment in Coventry, leaving them to focus not on medals but on the hope that the tournament has at least changed perceptions of this sport.

By beating Brazil in front of a crowd of 70,584 at Wembley, Hope Powell's team earned the kind of adulation and recognition that had eluded women's football in Britain for so long. But it also created a standard that they could not reach for a second time as they were outdone and occasionally outclassed by a strong Canada team.

With Britain showing signs of fatigue and sorely missing the injured Kelly Smith, Canada scored two early goals through Jonelle Filigno and Christine Sinclair. Britain rallied in the second half, but could not create a clear opportunity and were left to bemoan a costly mistake with nine minutes remaining, when the referee denied them what looked a clear penalty for Rhian Wilkinson's lunge on Eniola Aluko.

Canada deserved their lead. They had taken the game to Britain from the very start, repeatedly finding holes in and behind a midfield that had been so compact and resolute against Brazil. Canada were much more reserved in the second half, but it took until the final 20 minutes, after the introductions of Fara Williams, Rachel Williams and Rachel Yankey, for Britain to threaten. That compelling penalty appeal aside, there were few if-only moments.

At the end Stephanie Houghton, who scored in all three group games, wept and others fell to their knees while Powell and Smith went on to the pitch to console the defeated players. The coach pulled them together to lift their spirits before sending them to enjoy the appreciation of their crowd.

– Oliver Kay

Ben Ainslie
Finn class regatta

Down in Weymouth, another athlete seemed to be recovering his form and setting himself up for the medal podium once more.

Ben Ainslie won the final series race of the Finn class Olympic regatta with Jonas Hogh-Christensen, his rival from Denmark, in third place to give a huge boost to his quest for Olympic glory.

To win his fourth consecutive gold medal, Ainslie now needs only to beat Hogh-Christensen in the ten-boat, double-points medal race. The two are all but assured of gold and silver so long as Pieter-Jan Postma, of the Netherlands, does not beat Ainslie by more than six places and his rival by five.

When he came ashore after two of the most intense races of his career, it was immediately clear that Ainslie was relieved and was relishing the final shoot-out. He could put behind him his remarkable three-place gain on the last run of the penultimate race of the series that ensured he had the upper hand going into the finale. Now he can focus simply on keeping the Dane behind him for 30 minutes on the short, tight showcase Nothe course.

This medal race is short, sharp and places a huge premium on what happens on the start line and in the first few minutes. Ainslie has accumulated more hours in the Finn than most, built up hundreds of hours of match-race training and head-to-head racing over three America's Cup campaigns.

As he has shown throughout this regatta, Ainslie thrives most under pressure. 'It is a bit perverse but I quite like these situations,' Ainslie said with a smile. 'It is going to be really tough. Jonas has sailed really well all week.'

Ainslie is already assured of his fifth medal, colour to be decided, as are Iain Percy and Andrew Simpson in the Star. They take on Scheidt and Bruno Prada for gold tomorrow, leading into the final by a clear eight points.

Britain also head both the men's and women's 470 classes.

– Andi Robertson

GREAT BRITAIN
adidas
London 201
London

Wodjan Shaherkani
Judo

At around 10.30 in the morning, the ExCel Centre was no longer merely a venue for the opening rounds of the Olympic judo competition. For a few brief moments it became the nexus for powerful and incommensurable forces stretching from East to West. Feminism, human rights and religious fundamentalism collided on the mat, in addition to bodies and limbs.

Wodjan Shaherkani, an 18-year-old judoka, was greeted with a huge roar as she walked into the arena. She is not a great judo player and she lost in rapid time against Melissa Mojica, of Puerto Rico. But simply by fighting, by standing on the mat and doing battle, she created history as the first Saudi woman to compete at the Olympic Games.

Alongside Shaherkani, Sarah Attar, a 17-year-old living in California, will compete in the 800 metres. Neither athlete reached the qualifying standards, but they were both permitted to participate under the universality clause of the Olympic Charter.

Even then, the participation of Shaherkani was in doubt. The Saudi authorities insisted that she wear a head covering, which is against the rules of judo. A last-minute compromise was found and Shaherkani competed in a tight-fitting cap rather than the loose-fitting traditional hijab.

'I am happy to be at the Olympics,' she said afterwards. 'Unfortunately, we did not win a medal, but in the future we will and I will be a star for women's participation.' Of course, the raison d'être for the campaign by human rights groups was not about judo per se, nor the Olympics; it was about female liberation in one of the most restrictive states in the world. Saudi Arabia does not allow girls to take part in PE at state schools and there are no state programmes for women athletes and no female health clubs.

The backlash has been severe. When the two Saudi female athletes marched in the Opening Ceremony, an Arab hashtag that translates as 'prostitutes of the Olympics' emerged on Twitter. However, the participation of a teenage girl at the ExCel has put the position of Saudi women under the spotlight like never before.
– Matthew Syed

Michael Phelps
100 metres butterfly

Michael Phelps finished his individual swimming career with a golden jewel in the crown.

In the Aquatics Centre Michael Phelps claimed a remarkable victory in the final individual race of his career, winning the 100 metres butterfly in 51.21 seconds having been seventh at the turn.

It was the seventeenth Olympic gold medal of the American's career and his 21st of any colour. He will attempt to add one more to each tally in the men's 4 x 100 metres medley relay final, then retirement beckons for the 'Baltimore Bullet'.

For the first time in the history of the Games, the silver medal was shared in the event, Chad le Clos, of South Africa, and Evgeny Korotyshkin, of Russia, dead-heating in 51.44. Phelps turned the tables on Le Clos, the 20-year-old who had beaten him by 0.05 seconds five days ago in what had been the latter's signature race, the 200 metres butterfly.

The day after being denied by Le Clos, he was back at his best, defeating Ryan Lochte, his team-mate and the world champion, in the 200 metres individual medley to become the first man in history to win the same crown three times. This success made him the first to achieve the feat in two events.
– Craig Lord

Day 8 Round Up

BASKETBALL

Liz Cambage, of Australia, scored what was thought to be the first dunk in Olympic women's basketball history to help them to a 70–66 win against Russia in a battle of the teams ranked joint-second in the world. Australia's win left both teams with 3–1 records at the top of group B.

SHOOTING

James Huckle and Jonathan Hammond failed to make the final of the men's 50 metres rifle prone. Huckle, 22, from Essex, could not emulate his gold medal-winning room-mate Peter Wilson, shooting a below-par 591 out of 600 in qualifying. Hammond, 32, fared a little better by shooting 593, but he was still two points short of making the shoot-off.

DIVING

Hannah Starling, at 17 the youngest competitor in the event, was one place below the 18-diver limit when she stepped up to the board for her final dive– a forward 2½-somersault with a twist. Cheered on by the raucous support of the British fans in the Aquatics Centre, she produced her best effort of the day to scrape through in seventeenth – one place below Rebecca Gallantree, her team-mate.

TABLE TENNIS

Great Britain's women struggled from the outset in the team event as they lost 3–0 to the eighth seeds, North Korea. Joanna Parker, Kelly Sibley and Na Liu, Britain's three team members, were soundly beaten against opponents who are all above them in the ITTF rankings.

HANDBALL

Great Britain women's tough introduction to the Olympic Games continued as they slumped to a fourth successive group A defeat, going down 31–25, at the hands of Angola, to end any faint hopes of progressing to the quarter-finals.

Losses to Montenegro, Russia and Brazil in their opening three matches were par for the course, after the team's formation only six years ago, but they went into the day's opening encounter at the Copper Box with realistic hopes of beating the African champions, having done so in the test event in November.

MEDAL TABLE

				T
1. USA	21	10	12	43
2. CHINA	20	13	9	42
3. SOUTH KOREA	9	2	5	16
4. GREAT BRITAIN	8	6	8	22
5. FRANCE	8	5	6	19

TOP NATIONS: JUDO MEDALS IN NUMBERS

RUSSIA

12

(3G 1S 1B)

FRANCE

7

(2G 0S 5B)

SOUTH KOREA

3

(2G 0S 1B)

04.08.12
London 2012 Olympic Games
Day 9

Medals won by Team GB
Gold 6
Silver 1
Bronze 0

9

Fours, double sculls
Rowing

ON THE last day of finals at Eton Dorney, Great Britain won two gold medals and an eventful silver to complete their most successful Olympic rowing regatta. With nine medals overall, four of them gold, it beat the previous best haul of eight medals from the 1908 London Games. It also, by some way, surpassed the team's target for these Olympics of six medals.

The men's coxless four continued the country's success, then the newly formed lightweight women's double of Kat Copeland and Sophie Hosking won their first gold in only their fourth regatta together.

But Zac Purchase and Mark Hunter, who had looked on track for a third gold of the day in the

Below: Andrew Triggs Hodge, Tom James, Pete Reed and Alex Gregory celebrate their win at the end of a tough race.
Right: Kat Copeland and Sophie Hosking taste gold-medal success in the women's lightweight double sculls.

men's lightweight double, were passed in the last ten strokes by Denmark to add only a silver to the gold they had won in Beijing.

Their race had begun in drama. After only a few strokes, the British boat veered on to a buoy and Purchase stopped rowing. It turned out that there had been an equipment failure, with one of the clips that holds the seat on to its slide getting twisted and loosening a wheel. Since the fault happened within the first 100 metres, the rules allowed for the race to be restarted.

The race began again after a 15-minute delay. Britain took a one-second lead on Denmark, with New Zealand moving up fast, Britain had to fight on two fronts and were unable to prevent Denmark winning by a whisker.

Hunter lay prostrate on the pontoon afterwards, his chest heaving. There was massive disappointment at not defending their Olympic title, but they should be proud that having been sixth at the last two World Cups of the season, they had turned their form round so dramatically.

They did not see it that way. 'It hurt massively,' Hunter said. 'We feel we have let everybody down, but we gave everything we had. We only came for the gold and that was not what we got.'

'I'm completely gutted,' Purchase said. 'We'll spend days, weeks, months, the rest of our lives, trying to work out if we could have done more.'

The coxless four of Andrew Triggs Hodge, Tom James, Pete Reed and Alex Gregory, the first three champions in Beijing, led from the start in their

2km race but they were pushed all the way by Australia, who were never more than half a length behind. Britain won by half a length with the United States third.

'We fought bloody hard for that,' Hodge said. 'It is always a balance between technique and power, but that race was underpinned by some very effective brute force.'

If the men's four was almost expected to win, it was thought that the lightweight double of Copeland and Hosking would be scrapping for bronze at the start of the regatta. They had never competed together before this year and came into London 2012 with a record of one silver, a fourth and a fifth at this year's three World Cups. But they had shown in their heat and semi-final that they could be a force. With Hosking providing the rhythm from stroke and Copeland the engine in the bow, they moved well clear, leaving China to pip Greece to the silver medal on the line.

'All that hard work, it proves that it was worth the training and the sacrifices,' Hosking said. 'The last week has run so smoothly we even stopped talking about it. We knew what we were doing.'

Copeland was delightfully gobsmacked. 'I can't believe this is real,' she said. 'We're going to be on a stamp tomorrow.'

– Patrick Kidd

Women's cycling
Team pursuit

Laura Trott, Dani King and Jo Rowsell tore up the Velodrome and the record books to win gold for Team GB.

UNBELIEVABLE. AMAZING. The box of adjectives was empty as Great Britain's women's team pursuit squad took gold and shattered records on their way to glory in the Olympic Velodrome.

Laura Trott, Dani King and Jo Rowsell revealed themselves as not so much a team as a force of nature. Barely out of their teens – Trott is a mere 20, King, 21, and Rowsell the 23-year-old veteran – and among the most inexperienced riders at these Olympics, they have simply torn up record books and broken the hearts of their competitors.

It was exhausting, thrilling and just another night of exhilarating dominance for Great Britain in the Velodrome. That is four Olympic golds for Britain with plenty more in prospect.

These girls came to their home Olympics not just to win but to become legends. A remarkable trio, in five rides, they have broken the world record five times. In their first round in London, they shaved 0.051 seconds off their own world record they set in April, for a new benchmark of 3 minutes 15.669 seconds. But they were only warming up: in the penultimate round to reach the final, it was down to 3 minutes 14.682 seconds.

By the end of the first lap, the British girls had a lead of 0.481 seconds; by the finish, the trio were staring at Bausch's rear wheel, an astonishing 5.7 seconds ahead.

The scoreboard lit up 'New World Record' and suddenly women's cycling was in unexplored territory with a team pursuit record shattered and standing at 3 minutes 14.051 seconds. Yet Rowsell, Trott and King appeared barely to break sweat, their rhythm metronomic from first to last, relaxed and smooth.

At the end, the smiles were huge and the hugs extensive and not just for family, but for the team of extraordinary coaches who spotted the potential in these girls.

'Words cannot describe my feelings,' King said. 'I don't think this smile will come off my face for a long time.' Rowsell added: 'It hasn't sunk in yet. Things have just got better and better. The spirit in the team is fantastic and we have taken inspiration from the crowd. They have been fantastic and spurred us on. We were always confident but we didn't take it for granted. We knew we had work to do. But I had confidence in the girls right from the start.'

It was the end of another glorious day that started as it was meant to finish. Jason Kenny started the ball rolling. In the first round of the men's cycling sprint, he roared to a new Olympic record. Kenny already has a gold medal in the team event, but he is looking for his moment of individual glory.

Kenny, 24, was picked ahead of Sir Chris to raised eyebrows but then proved his point in 9.7 seconds of pedalling early on Saturday morning to set his record to put himself emphatically into the last eight of the sprint. He goes into Monday's finals as favourite.

The cheers had not stopped, though. Ed Clancy, 27, is halfway through his gruelling omnium of six different events and will hope to be among the medal winners when it finally comes to an end. He was leading after the sprint and points race and looking in the sort of inspired form that is the hallmark of Team GB's cycling squad at these home Olympics.

– Kevin Eason

ENNIS

Jessica Ennis
Heptathlon

Jessica Ennis, running her way to Olympic gold and into the record books.

IT WOULD BE hard to find a more perfect icon for these Olympic Games than Jessica Ennis, who won the gold medal in the heptathlon. Ennis clocked 2 minutes 8.65 seconds in the 800 metres to seal the victory. It gave her 6,955 points and a new British record.

She did it in swashbuckling style, too. Having gone out fast, she was overhauled by two rivals, including Tatyna Chernova, the world champion. Not one for doing things by halves, Ennis responded off the final bend, sending a corner of London mad, and cemented her place in both sporting history and a nation's affections.

Chernova ended up a distant third with Lilli Schwarzkopf of Germany, second. Britain's Katarina Johnson-Thompson, 19 years old and tipped to be as good as Ennis one day, was a wonderful fourteenth.

Ennis collapsed, held her head and cried. She picked up a flag, tried to high-five her coach, Toni Minichiello, in the stands, and went on a raucous lap of honour.

Ennis knew she probably had the gold medal wrapped up before she even set foot on this blisteringly fast track for the final 800 metres. It was a dream scenario. She had the heptathlon all but won in five events. She won by a huge margin. She chalked up three personal bests in three individual disciplines.

The competition ended up being surprisingly straightforward. Ennis started the second day 184 points ahead of Austra Skujyte, of Lithuania, and with the two women she most feared, Chernova and Ukraine's Nataliya Dobrynska, way back. Nevertheless, her two weakest events remained, the long jump and the javelin.

When she opened the first day with a sorry long jump of 5.95 metres, while Chernova quickly got to 6.54 metres, nerves jangled. But as the pressure mounted she jumped 6.40 metres, the baseline distance she craved, and then increased it to 6.48 metres. Suddenly Chernova needed a wonder throw and Ennis needed to throw like an apathetic darts player. The gold medal was effectively won there and then.

The javelin just underlined her fighting spirit. Back in South Korea, at those ill-fated World Championships, she had managed only 39.95 metres and Chernova took her title. Ennis buried those ghosts by throwing a personal best of 47.49 metres. It was her third personal best of this heptathlon and meant that if she could run the 800 metres in 2 minutes 7 seconds she would break her own British record. Chernova managed only 46.29 metres. Ennis had beaten the world champion in six out of seven events, which is about as decisive as it gets. It was victory by a country mile.

Johnson-Thompson has been a breath of fresh air and has clearly relished the Olympic experience as a teenage dreamer should. Some sagacious onlookers believe she will be better than Ennis one day. If Ennis sticks around then the Rio Olympics could be twice as good. Johnson-Thompson's score of 6,267 points was a personal best.

The highlight for Ennis, other than the finale, will have been the first event. Her hurdles was stunning, her time of 12.54 seconds matching the time that won gold in Beijing in 2008. That time has been beaten by only two women this year and was a British record to go with the one she shares in the high jump.

Ennis's panoramic smile has sometimes masked the fact this has been a hard journey. Four years ago she broke her ankle and missed the Olympics. Two years ago she needed a brain scan and the Epley manoeuvre to combat a debilitating attack of dizziness. Her down-to-earth family has helped her through the hard times, losing two world titles in the last seven months. She lives with her long-term boyfriend Andy in Sheffield – they are due to get married next year – and always declines to go warm-weather training, preferring to stay at home in the battle-hardening cold.

'I worry a lot,' she says. 'If I could change anything about myself then it would be that. I can control it, but things would be better if I could just stop. It's not only sport, it's everything. It's not worrying to the extreme that I'm rocking in my chair, but I suppose it's strange that I can then go out and compete. I think I was naïve back then, blissfully training and thinking life was always sweet. That injury opened my eyes up to everything. It made me realize how freak things can affect your season and career.'

Now she has little to worry about. Nice girls need not finish last and Britain have never had a more popular track and field gold medal-winner.
– *Rick Broadbent*

adidas

Greg Rutherford
Long jump

If Jessica Ennis was the athlete Britain both yearned and expected to take gold, then Greg Rutherford was the athlete who rather more quietly took glory. The world No 1 won gold in the long jump and became the first British man to do so since Lynn Davies in 1964.

Two Brits were in contention: Rutherford, from Milton Keynes, and Chris Tomlinson. Both qualified in top-five positions for the final, with Tomlinson two centimetres behind his British team-mate. With Irving Saladino, the reigning Olympic champion, failing to make the final after three no-jumps, a British medal was a real possibility. Rutherford, however, had been too prone to injury to allow anyone to pin home Games hopes on him. His first jump went slightly awry while Tomlinson set the standard with a distance of 8.06 metres.

With his second jump Rutherford stretched to 8.21 metres and the Brits were, briefly, dominating. The hope was they would see-saw their way through right to the very end. Tomlinson jumped 7.87 metres with his second attempt, which kept him behind Will Claye, the American, and then Sebastian Bayer of Germany. Tomlinson took the bronze position with an 8.07 metres achieved with trademark pace. Claye maintained the pressure with an 8.12 metres.

And then, while the crowd were screaming for Jess Ennis as she lined up in the 800 metres, almost unnoticed, Rutherford leapt to 8.31 metres.

Tomlinson, meanwhile, was starting to slip down the rankings. Going into the final round Rutherford led despite fouling on his fifth attempt. Tomlinson was ready and eager for his final jump but was forced to abort his effort for a few minutes because of the distractions surrounding the start of the men's 10,000 metres final. The resulting jump was nothing special. He finished sixth overall. Claye mucked up his final leap so that Rutherford could jump for fun knowing he was already Olympic champion. It was a dreadful effort, but who cared? It was gold for Britain. Again. Mitchell Watt, from Australia, took silver with 8.16 metres and Claye took bronze with 8.12 metres.

'You can't just turn up and expect it to happen,' Tomlinson had said of the home crowd factor. It failed to inspire him sufficiently but Rutherford sparkled.

– Alyson Rudd

Mo Farah
10,000 metres

Mo Farah capped a great day for the nation's athletes when he became the first British man to win the Olympic 10,000 metres title.

'I can't believe it,' an emotional Farah said. 'The crowd just got behind me and it got louder and louder. It's the best moment of my life. Long distance is a lonely event and you get out what you put in.'

Farah had to overcome some rough tactics from the African runners, who ganged up on him, but the Somalia-born star took the lead with a lap to go and then, when push came to shove, left everyone else trailing. Farah celebrated with his trademark 'Mobot' dance and then hugged his stepdaughter Rihanna, who had run onto the track.

Farah crossed the line in 27 minutes 30.42 seconds to underscore his status as the greatest distance runner in the world. The Africans had tried to run a tactical race, speeding up, slowing down and even barging Farah. They knew they needed to break him. An Eritrean duo bumped into him, and the Bekele brothers, Kenenisa and Tariku, tried to make it a fast race to negate the advantage of the Briton's sprint finish.

It was a real test of Farah's nerve as the field lapped in 61 seconds before the halfway stage. However, he kept his cool and was helped by his training partner, the USA's Galen Rupp, who came through for the silver ahead of Tariku Bekele. The elder Bekele, never beaten in a 10,000 metres race he had finished, was fourth. That Farah ran the last lap in 53 seconds shows how good he is.

Farah's journey to the Olympic stage has been a meandering one, which matched the erratic tactics he used to employ before he got serious, lived with the Kenyans and then teamed up with Albert Salazar, a Cuba-born American.

Four years ago Farah went out in the semi-finals of the Beijing Olympics and then finished seventh at the World Championships in Berlin two years ago. It seemed he would be remembered only as another man who went down fighting, the next best thing rather than the next big one.

Now he favours underwater treadmills and barefoot running, but the partnership, which has involved Farah uprooting his young family to move to Portland, Oregon to train on the Nike university campus, has clearly worked.

– Rick Broadbent

Previous page: Greg Rutherford jumping his way to victory and becoming the first British man to win gold since 1964.
Opposite: The moment Mo Farah had worked so hard for stopped him in his tracks.

adidas
TEAM GB
GREAT BRITAIN
London 2012
FARAH
adidas
TEAM GB

‘The crowd just got behind me and it got louder and louder. It’s the best moment of my life.’
Mo Farah

Mo Farah celebrates his win with his now-trademark ‘mobot’ pose, while Greg Rutherford soaks up the cheers of the delighted crowd.

Day 9 Round Up

TENNIS
At Wimbledon, Andy Murray, who meets Roger Federer in the men's final, also won through to the final of the mixed doubles with Laura Robson.

ATHLETICS
Christine Ohuruogu, the defending champion, qualified for the finals of the 400 metres with a season best of 50.22 seconds.

Dwain Chambers' 12-year wait to get back to the Olympics after overturning his lifetime ban for doping began with victory in his 100-metre heat in 10.02 seconds.

Shelly-Ann Fraser-Pryce of Jamaica retained the women's 100-metre title, winning in 10.75 seconds. She became the first woman since American Gail Devers (1992 and 1996) to win two 100-metre titles in a row at the Olympic Games.

BADMINTON
China's second seeds, Tian Qing and Zhao Yunlei, won the women's badminton doubles, beating Japan's fourth seeds, Mizuki Fujii and Reika Kakiiwa, 21–10, 25–23.

MEDAL TABLE

				T
1. USA	26	13	15	54
2. CHINA	25	16	12	53
3. GREAT BRITAIN	14	7	8	29
4. SOUTH KOREA	9	3	5	17
5. FRANCE	8	6	8	22

LONG JUMP: MEN'S FINAL

Gold GBR

8.31

Silver AUS

8.16

Bronze USA

8.12

05.08.12
London 2012 Olympic Games
Day 10

Medals won by Team GB
Gold 2
Silver 4
Bronze 2

10

Andy Murray
Men's tennis singles

AFTER THE spectacular events of Super Saturday, Britain dared not hope for a repeat performance, but many couldn't help but will on one particular athlete. For Andy Murray, this final was not just about winning Olympic gold, it was about healing the hurt of the Wimbledon final a few weeks ago.

The purple podium had been placed on Centre Court, the men's singles medal-winners were walking to their spots and, his head still in the clouds, Andy Murray strolled past where he should have stopped until Roger Federer gestured him to his proper place. That was the kind of unforgettable day this was, of incredulity mixed with joy, of gestures both great and small, of great deeds and chivalry, of Murray peering at his reflection in a gold medal.

This was the moment. He had looked for it, worked for it, played his heart out in its pursuit, taken savage knocks, buckled, shed tears and then, on the court that has a resonance in tennis nowhere can match, it happened for him. Not in a grand-slam tournament, but after this they will seem that little less daunting. This was that once-in-a-lifetime, the Olympic Games, at Wimbledon, and this time, all the dreams came true.

Murray won 6–2, 6–1, 6–4, a victory margin staggering in its severity and wondrous in its execution. The nation – and that means every nation that goes to make up these islands – was as one in saluting him. As the British flag was raised above this Centre Court, only the most hard-hearted would not have felt like rejoicing.

Britain last won a singles gold medal at tennis in 1908, when the 37-year-old Major (his real first name) Ritchie defeated German Otto Froitzheim, who tried to play the Englishman from the back of the court but was beaten in straight sets.

Murray dropped only one set in the entire event, his performances both against Novak Djokovic and Federer were of a breathtakingly high standard. As Murray walked to serve for gold, he looked to have gone pale – but that image was false. The blood was pumping and the last two points, both aces, scattered all the doubts.

As he captured the moment on his video camera, Murray's father, Will, melted when he saw his son's head tip forward to receive his medal. 'Who would have a thought a skinny wee boy from Dunblane would win an Olympic gold medal?'
– Neil Harman

Andy Murray is overcome as he realises he has put aside his recent defeat on Centre Court to take home the gold medal.

Andy Murray and Laura Robson

Mixed tennis doubles

MURRAY WAS back on court just a few hours later with his mixed doubles partner, Laura Robson, for another attempt at gold.

Robson would not have played at these Olympic Games at all had she not been awarded a 'special exempt' into the women's doubles, another player pulled out of the singles, which gave her a shot at that, and Andy Murray had not selected her to be his partner in the mixed. It is amazing how life can turn in a few days.

That after all this she was frustrated to have won only a silver medal speaks volumes about the depths of her ambition. Walking away from a loss to Max Mirnyi and Victoria Azarenka, the No 1 seeds from Belarus, Robson was in no mood for congratulatory pats on the back. She wanted gold and she went very close to helping a gold medal-winner claim another.

For the third time in succession, the British pair had to win a champions' tie-break to win the match, but this time Mirnyi and Azarenka prevailed 2–6, 6–3 (10–8).

She had sat through the latter stages of her partner's stunning victory in the singles behind Judy, Murray's mother. 'It was nerve-racking because she was constantly talking and I was just trying to calm myself down,' she said. 'But this has been one of the best weeks of my life.'

The same was true of Murray, who came good in the finest possible style to become an Olympic champion. He had spent the previous night glued to the television watching Britain win gold after gold. 'I thought that Mo Farah, especially, was unbelievable,' Murray said. 'He ran the last of 25 laps in 52 seconds and when I am completely fresh I can't do it in better than 57.

'I just wanted to be a part of this success, the atmosphere has been incredible, everyone has been so happy, so pumped and I'm just glad I've been able to contribute to that.'

Inevitably, he was asked the question about whether he would swap gold for the Wimbledon title. 'I wouldn't change this for anything right now,' he said. 'I hope that this victory will help me become an even better player.'

– Neil Harman

Ben Ainslie

Sailing

AFTER A WEEK of high emotions, another British hopeful at last put his supporters out of their misery when he secured the gold he had been striving for, and which at times had seemed out of his reach.

Victory for Ben and victory for *Rita* on the still waters of Weymouth Harbour. The most successful partnership between man and sailboat since Nelson died at Trafalgar has come to an end. After gold medals at the past three Olympics, Ben Ainslie and his Finn dinghy will not race together again.

While many sailors are fickle, moving from boat to boat every couple of years, Ainslie has stayed loyal to *Rita* for nine years. He sends her off to a maritime museum as a four-er, the greatest Olympic sailor there has been. While Ainslie teased us by suggesting that he might be there in Rio de Janeiro he will not be seen in a solo dinghy again. The world of dinghy sailing is changing and Ainslie had to fight off a stiff challenge for his place in the British team from Giles Scott, who is just as talented but ten years younger and, at 6ft 5in, six inches taller.

'We're the last generation of guys who are not 6ft 4in,' Jonas Hogh-Christensen, 31, said. 'We barely made it here. There are a lot of guys pushing and in four years' time they will be four years stronger and we will be four years older.'

Hogh-Christensen beat Ainslie in the first six races of this regatta, but then made the naive error last week of making the Englishman angry by claiming, with Pieter-Jan Postma, the Dutch sailor, that Ainslie had clipped a mark. Ainslie denied it, but took a penalty turn rather than risk disqualification and then announced that he would get his revenge for being dobbed in to the teachers.

Afterwards, Ainslie said that it was all water under the bridge. 'It's racing, it happens a lot,' he said. 'We have a lot of respect for each other. I was seriously worried after six races. Jonas was fast and I knew something had to change.' By the medal race, he had got back into the competition to such an extent that he only had to finish ahead of Hogh-Christensen to claim the gold. That was until Postma made his own attempt to change the story by charging through the field to third place on the final beat.

If the Dutchman had made it into second place, he could have denied Ainslie gold with the Englishman preoccupied with covering Hogh-Christensen. Fortunately, he pushed too hard, took a penalty and tailed off in the closing stages. 'My heart was in my mouth all the way round,' Ainslie said. 'It was a difficult race on that course and hard to predict when the wind is that shifty and puffy.'

Hogh-Christensen took the advantage off the start, but Ainslie, known as 'the wind whisperer' for his innate ability to sense where conditions may be more favourable, headed down the right of the course, with eight of his nine rivals going left, and was able to find a breeze that moved him ahead of his rival at the top mark. He flew down the first downwind straight and moved into second

Ben Ainslie lights his flare to celebrate winning his fourth Olympic gold medal.

‘Ben is the best sailor in the world across all classes. What he has done is a great achievement and should be applauded.’ Hogh-Christensen

place but in trying to stay with Hogh-Christensen dropped to ninth, with the Dane tenth, which is how they finished, Jonathan Lobert, of France, took advantage to stretch away from the fleet to win the race and take the bronze medal from Postma.

Hogh-Christensen is the first Danish sailor to win a medal in the Olympic Finn class since Henning Wind in 1964. Ainslie now has four golds and a silver. ‘Ben is the best sailor in the world across all classes,’ Hogh-Christensen said. ‘What he has done is a great achievement and should be applauded.’ And applaud they did, long and hard from the beaches around Weymouth Harbour.
– *Patrick Kidd*

Christine Ohuruogu
400 metres

WHILE OTHER members of Team GB ecstatically finished their Games clutching their Olympic medals with sheer elation, for one athlete, silver was not only not good enough, but it was a devastating blow.

As in her life, so in the race, Christine Ohuruogu won silver in the 400 metres, chasing down a game that had long before seemed to have left her behind.

To know how far Ohuruogu has come, you have to remember where she was this time a year ago. Then, she had become a bit of a relic of her golden Beijing age; she was the Olympic champion who looked nothing of the sort.

She settled into the blocks in Daegu, South Korea, at the World Championships, jumped the gun and was disqualified. That embarrassing early exit prompted questions: anyone remember a 400 metre runner false-starting? And: is this the last we will see of her as a competitive runner?

The answer to the second question has been delivered comprehensively here at her home Games. She is, of course, the real home-town girl, the most home town the GB team could find. She was brought up in Newham, a mile away from where this stadium now lies. The motivation to be the

In a thrilling burst of speed, Christine Ohuruogu ran a race that was fast enough for silver, but not fast enough for her liking.

Ohuruogu of old and not the Christine O of Daegu could hardly have been more compelling.

What we always knew of Ohuruogu, we saw again. She had run under 50 seconds only twice in her life, once in 2007 when she became World Champion and then in Beijing when she took that Olympic title. What she has been a master at is timing her season to perfection.

And likewise here. The strong favourite was Sanya Richards-Ross, of the United States – she runs sub-50 seconds all the time. So here, she took off fast, closing down on Ohuruogu, halfway down the back straight. But Richards-Ross was not alone in going past her. As they went into the top bend, the rest of the field engulfed her. With 80 metres to go, Ohuruogu was seventh, but that was when she started chasing down the opposition.

Ohuruogu's strength is her finish and her late burst was thrilling. One by one, she reeled in those in front of her, with 20 metres to go, she was fourth, but then she went past Amantle Montsho and, at the line, DeeDee Trotter.

Ahead of her still was Richards-Ross, the one she could not catch, and on the screen was her time: 49.70 seconds, her third time under 50 seconds, her third world or Olympic medal. This extraordinary outcome, though, was not quite extraordinary enough for herself. 'I was stunned,' she said. 'I was heartbroken. To lose your title like that. I tightened up. I could feel my shoulders lifting, it is really hard to control when you are under fatigue. The line came too soon. But I always came here with one thing only: to continue my reign as Olympic champ.'
– *Owen Slot*

Louis Smith
Gymnastics

WE ARE GORGING on so much lovely gold that sometimes we forget that silver, too, can be fabulous.

Silver certainly felt great around the neck of Louis Smith. Silver was brilliant even though it came in what seemed the most agonising of circumstances, when Smith finished on the same score as Krisztian Berki in the final of the men's pommel horse.

Both were awarded 16.066, but the Hungarian took gold because he had a higher mark for execution, with Smith marginally higher for difficulty. Those seemed the circumstances for tears and heartache, but Smith was full of class and generosity, happy for Berki. 'It would be easy to say I would have liked an extra tenth from the judges, but that's a big thing. It would have crushed someone else's dream,' Smith, 23, said. 'I'm happy. I've come second to one of the best pommel horse gymnasts the world has ever seen.'

Smith had been working on a 7.1, with three Russians on a single handle, but no one had attempted it in an Olympic final. Smith says he has a 30 per cent success rate. There was another problem. 'My hardest routine wasn't going the way I wanted in the warm-up,' he said. 'So I went for the 7.' He was convinced this middle way was the right decision as he took to the pommel, and even more convinced once he finished a routine he ranked as the best of his life.

So, any regrets? 'I am very happy with my choice.' Smith said. 'If you watch the routines back in slow motion, you'd see the best person won.'
– Matt Dickinson

Whitlock (in blue) wowed the crowd and the judges to win a surprise bronze medal, while Louis Smith put in a slick performance which earned him silver in the same event.

Max Whitlock
Gymnastics

FOUR YEARS AGO Louis Smith became a household name courtesy of winning a bronze medal in artistic gymnastics. On Day 10, Max Whitlock replicated the feat, on the same piece of apparatus.

Thanks to Smith, the teenager's success is seen as part of a bigger, glorious picture for British gymnastics, but only those inside the sport had an inkling that he was capable of taking a medal in the pommel horse final.

This was Whitlock's second leading competition – he was part of the silver medal-winning team at the Commonwealth Games two years ago – and the 19-year-old was a reserve for the World Championships in Tokyo last year. But he caught the eye in the gymnastics test event and has been funnelled through various competitions to discover how consistent he could be under pressure.

'He came through with flying colours every time,' Eddie van Hoof, technical director for the men's programme, said. 'And we were totally confident that Max would compete here in the Greenwich Arena and contribute to the team.'

Whitlock, from Hemel Hempstead, made a small error in the qualification round and scraped into the final, in which he scored 15.6.

'But we knew that if he went really clean we had a chance of two people getting a medal,' Van Hoof said. 'He has a little cheekiness to him, but he's quite quiet normally, an introvert, a real thinker who put in the work and has been rewarded.'

Much was made of which routine Smith would choose to perform in his efforts to outshine Krisztian Berki, of Hungary, his great rival, but there were no such complications for Whitlock. His routine was fixed: the only slight, potential variation was on the dismount but the intention was always to go for the more difficult one that he had been executing consistently for six months.

The unlikely story of British excellence in artistic gymnastics is likely to become even more astonishing when Beth Tweddle and Kristian Thomas go into action. We all know about Tweddle and her attempt to add Olympic gold to her three World Championship titles. That Thomas could take gold is much more of a surprise. He has a new routine on the vault and was superb in qualifying but stumbled in the men's final.

The general view is that his routine is so tricky that if he executes it cleanly, winning a medal is just a formality.

– Alyson Rudd

Usain Bolt
100 metres

At London 2012 there were always going to be some athletes you could count on to wow the crowds and who would leave their fellow competitors far behind, resignedly shaking their heads in awe at their performances. In the 100 metres, those athletes were the Jamaicans.

Usain Bolt turned back time, stopped the clock and made the world suspend its disbelief once more as the fastest phenomenon in history proved the man of the moment.

In what many felt was a wide-open race, Bolt closed off all avenues of dissent. He clocked an Olympic record of 9.63 seconds, the second fastest run of all time, with Yohan Blake second in 9.75 seconds and Justin Gatlin a tainted third in a lifetime best of 9.79 seconds.

A stellar cast-list of heroes and villains produced one of the most jaw-dropping feats of blink-and-you-miss-it brilliance. 'Usain, Usain, Usain,' they chanted down at the London love-in. How they lapped up all the drama as Bolt became the first man to retain the 100 metres title.

We knew Bolt was good and great and a demigod. We did not know that he was a master of misdirection, pulling the wool over the eyes of those who said he was injured or could not start.

There were no half-measures in the semi-finals, with seven of eight qualifiers running under ten seconds on a state-of-the-art track whose beneficence has seen it dubbed the magic carpet. There was Bolt, the triple world record-holder and triple Olympic champion, and there was Blake, the world champion and the man who would be king. In the US's red, white and blue corner stood Tyson Gay, the second fastest man in history. Add Asafa Powell, a former world record-holder, and Ryan Bailey, a former gang member who was once stabbed in the leg three times, and there were candidates and subplots enough to make this the greatest race in history.

The main protagonist was always Bolt. The big question was just how serious the hamstring strain was that forced him out of a pre-Olympic meeting. Could he get back to his best and make 80,000 believers of the Olympic Congregation?

The 100 metres is a race of broad scope and fine margins, though, and so Blake was installed as favourite. The talent in this race was evinced by the fact Gay has barely been mentioned in the countdown to what he and Bolt hoped would be catharsis.

Meanwhile, the threat of Gatlin lingered like a cancer over this final. Repentance has to be a precursor to redemption, but Gatlin is a man who represents the bad old days.

'Everybody is bored with the Bolt Show,' Gatlin had boasted after clocking an impressive

Usain Bolt blows away the competition again, to retain his Olympic 100 metres title in breathtaking speed and style.

9.87 seconds in Doha in May. He may have been right, but few people would have preferred to watch the further exploits of a man who has already left one Olympic title infused with the whiff of suspicion. Of course, some would suggest Gatlin's 2004 crown should remain untarnished because it was before he tested positive in 2006.

However, seeing him line up against Bolt told you everything you needed to know about the pernicious osmosis of doping. Bolt has never failed a test, never done anything to harm his sport, never done anything to deserve the sort of gossip and innuendo that any great athletic feat now provokes due to a timeline of cheats. Some will say that Dwain Chambers is just as bad as Gatlin, but at least he coughed up. He ran 10.04 seconds in his heat, lining up next to Bolt, and missed the final by two places.

Adam Gemili also failed to make what would have been a frankly astonishing final. The former footballer from Dartford clocked 10.06 seconds and can go home from his 'bonus' Olympics satisfied in the knowledge he was eleventh best in the world at the age of 18. Even Bolt did not manage that.

– *Rick Broadbent*

Ed Clancy

Omnium

THE BRITISH RUN of success at the Velodrome continued on Day 10, as Ed Clancy won bronze in the omnium, sparking yet more jubilant scenes in the home camp.

This was a second medal of the Games for Clancy, who was part of the team pursuit squad, and the real beauty of it was that it was viewed as a bonus, a medal that they had not counted on in their weighty collection. For all their attention to detail, the Britain team have always viewed the omnium – a new Olympic event, incorporating six races over two days – with a certain suspicion, owing to the unpredictable nature of the points race, the elimination race and the scratch race.

Like the rest of the Britain team, Clancy has hit top form at precisely the right time for these Games. Going into the final event of the omnium in fifth place, Clancy recorded a remarkably quick time in the 1km time trial. His time of 1 minute 00.981 seconds was only 0.27 seconds outside the Olympic record for specialists in the event, set by Chris Hoy at the Athens Games in 2004.

Clancy then had to sit and wait for the final four riders to complete their time trials, which he did with a cold towel over his head, utterly spent. When the scoreboard flashed up the final standings, showing that Clancy had won the time trial and finished third overall behind Lasse Hansen, of Denmark, and Bryan Coquard, of France, he was mobbed by the British coaches.

Starting the day in fourth place after three events, Clancy finished second in the 4km individual pursuit, then had a difficult time in the 15km scratch race, finishing tenth. But his performance in the 'kilo' was very strong. The rumours are that the omnium may be dropped for the 2016 Games and the kilo reinstated. 'If the kilo comes back,' Dave Brailsford, performance director of British Cycling said, 'Ed Clancy will win it.'

Riding six events in two days in the immediate aftermath of the team pursuit may be a challenge, but the hardest part for Clancy was being unable to celebrate the gold medal with his team-mates. 'Getting up in the morning when team-mates are lying in bed fully clothed with hangovers, walking past the carnage on the floor was tough,' he said. So was he planning to make up for lost time? 'Definitely,' he said.
– *John Westerby*

Ed Clancy finishes the final leg of the six-part omnium to take another bronze for Britain's cycling team.

Day 10 Round Up

EQUESTRIANISM
Superb opening rounds from Nick Skelton on Big Star and Ben Maher on Tripple X put the Great Britain showjumping team in the silver-medal position, level with the Netherlands, Sweden and Switzerland, at the end of the first round of the team competition at Greenwich Park.

TRIATHLON
Great Britain's hopes of a first Olympic medal in the sport rest on the Brownlee brothers, Alistair and Jonathan, after Helen Jenkins finished fifth in a dramatic women's race and said that she had been carrying an injury.

Jenkins needed several painkillers because of a knee injury suffered diving ten weeks ago. After two hours, the race for gold came down to a sprint between Nicola Spirig, of Switzerland, and Lisa Nordén, of Sweden. They appeared to have broken the tape together, but a photo revealed that Spirig had won by centimetres, with Erin Densham, of Australia, taking bronze.

BADMINTON
China completed an unprecedented sweep of all five of the sport's Olympic gold medals after Cai Yun and Fu Haifeng won the men's doubles title at Wembley Arena. Shortly after Lin Dan had defeated Lee Chong Wei, of Malaysia, to win the men's singles title, Cai and Fu beat Mathias Boe and Carsten Mogensen, of Denmark, 21–16, 21–15.

HOCKEY
James Tindall crowned a thrilling second-half comeback by Great Britain when he hammered in the equaliser four minutes from time after the team fought back from 3–0 down to draw with Australia. Britain's last group game is against Spain and a draw could be enough to reach the semi-finals. The Netherlands beat Germany, the Olympic champions, 3–1, to win pool B.

MEDAL TABLE

				T
1. CHINA	30	17	14	61
2. USA	28	14	18	60
3. GREAT BRITAIN	16	11	10	37
4. SOUTH KOREA	10	4	6	20
5. FRANCE	8	8	9	25

9.63

Usain Bolt's time in the 100m final.

06.08.12
London 2012 Olympic Games
Day 11

Medals won by Team GB
Gold 2
Silver 0
Bronze 1

11

Jason Kenny
Individual sprint

Baugé tried but just couldn't keep up with the new king of the track, and Jason Kenny sprinted home to gold and glory.

DAY 11 BROUGHT the expectation of more medals in the Velodrome, and for Jason Kenny it was a nervous journey onto the track as he prepared to compete without his team-mates for the first time in these Games.

The enormity of the moment struck Kenny as he was about to ride for gold and glory. Kenny was leading 1–0 against Grégory Baugé, a Frenchman previously regarded as invincible. One more victory and he would claim Olympic sprint champion Sir Chris Hoy's title.

'I hadn't thought about the pressure until the very last ride,' Kenny said. 'But then I thought, "If Chris was in my shoes, there is no way he would lose this one."' Kenny was not just racing a hulking Frenchman, the reigning world champion, but riding to justify his inclusion ahead of Hoy. He was racing against the legend.

All the more kudos to Kenny, then, that he should have produced such a brilliant victory that will have filled Hoy with pride, as well as the rest of Britain.

Hoy in 2008, now Kenny in 2012 – though we should probably leave the comparisons there.

This was Kenny's first individual gold medal, his other two coming in team sprints in Beijing and London, and you might think that he would love the idea of striking out on his own, stepping out of Hoy's giant shadow. Instead, Kenny said that he had been missing his mates in the past few days. 'It's been lonely training on my own,' he said.

He wished that Hoy had been able to compete with him, as they did in Beijing when Kenny took silver behind the knight of the track. But the UCI had changed the rules to one rider per country. Because of those rules, Dave Brailsford, the head of British cycling, and Shane Sutton, the head coach, had to choose between Hoy and Kenny – a ridiculous position to be put in given the calibre of both men – and they went with the younger man.

Hoy, 36, had not grumbled and he tweeted a good luck message to his young team-mate, adding: 'Not that he'll need any help. He's flying!' So it proved. Kenny easily beat Njisane Phillip, of Trinidad and Tobago, while Baugé put away Shane Perkins, of Australia, the eventual bronze medal-winner, in his semi-final.

This was the clash that 6,000 fans had come to see; a gladiatorial battle on wheels between the World Champion and the young British contender. Kenny had never beaten Baugé, losing to him in World Championship finals in 2011 and 2012 (though being awarded the former when Baugé missed doping tests).

But Kenny's record in qualifying was a good form guide. 'We realised that we had a bit more speed, which is always a luxury,' Kenny said. 'If you don't make mistakes you should come out on top nine times out of ten.' Yet speed is not enough to win the individual sprint. It is about timing, tactics, and bluff. A game of poker played at 70kmph.

Baugé led out the first race. Kenny claimed that he rode poorly, but that is not how it seemed to 6,000 screaming fans as he came around the outside and took the Frenchman on the line.

Then came that moment of nerves when he thought of Hoy. 'If you look back on history, if it comes down to that really important ride, he has that killer instinct.' So did Kenny. This time he was leading, and he struck out early in the final lap. Baugé never came close to catching him. It was a stunning triumph.

Victory put Kenny high on the list of British Olympians, behind only the Mount Rushmore legends of Hoy, Redgrave, Wiggins, Ainslie, Pinsent and Radmilovic. But nothing has changed him. He just likes riding his bike. 'It was great to enjoy the crowd and soak it up,' he said. 'I didn't savour the moment after the team sprint because I felt so sick. I was trying to keep my lunch down.'
– *Matt Dickinson*

adidas
BRITAIN
TEAM GB

GREAT BRI
AT BRITAIN

Equestrian team
Showjumping

IT HAS BEEN 60 years since Britain last won showjumping gold, which made the equestrian team's well-deserved success on Day 11 all the sweeter. Britain's showjumping team, led by Nick Skelton and Big Star, brought home the team gold after a sensational performance in which they fended off a strong challenge from the Netherlands in a thrilling final jump-off.

It was the first medal the team have won since a silver in 1984 and Skelton, 54, said: 'I've waited 54 years for this. It means everything. It's huge for the country and it's huge for me – I was running out of time.'

At the start of the day, Britain were tied in the silver-medal position with the Netherlands, Switzerland and Sweden on four faults, behind Saudi Arabia, the surprise leaders on a single fault. The 13-fence course that Bob Ellis had designed for this final round was big, technical and described as 'very difficult'.

Skelton, who has not come even close to touching a single pole with Beverley and Gary Widdowson's nine-year-old stallion Big Star, made light of the technical questions asked, producing his third clear round of the week with consummate ease.

Ben Maher, 29, on Tripple X, looked about to follow suit until they rolled a pole at the tenth fence to come home with four faults.

With the Netherlands producing a clear round from their second rider, Scott Brash, 26, instead of finding himself 'cushioned' as the third rider to jump for Britain, was put in the hot seat, needing a clear round to keep the team in the hunt.

Peter Charles, 52, Britain's last rider, brought hope of the team finishing on a zero score (the best three riders' scores count), only to have a pole down at Fence 12 and have a time fault, to come home with five faults. With Gerco Schroder, the top Dutch rider, still to come on his horse London, it looked as if Britain would have to settle for silver.

As the Dutchman gathered up the reins to begin his round, the crowd, busy working out the maths, fell silent. Clear over the first six fences he approached the combination Fence 7, one of the most influential fences on the course, and to gasps from the crowd the middle pole fell. Both teams were now on eight faults: a jump-off would decide who got gold.

A frenzied few minutes followed in the press area, with contradictory messages as to whether it would be all four riders jumping or only one from each team. Finally an authoritative British voice rang out: 'It's all to go again – the British riders are warming up.' In the event of a tie on faults, the fastest times would win.

Skelton – first in over a shortened eight-fence course – produced a fast clear round in 47.27 seconds. The chase was on. Jur Vrieling on Bubalu were clear but a fraction slower. Maher then brilliantly compensated for his earlier mistake with a clear round, faster than Vrieling's. Brash had one mistake but that was cancelled out by faults from both Maikel van der Vleuten on Verdi and Marc Houtzager on Sterrehof's Tamino. With two clear rounds by Britain in the bag, a third would secure the gold.

So Charles would have to echo Harry Llewellyn's final round on Foxhunter in 1952 when, after a disappointing first round, the gold had depended on him jumping clear in the second. His face taut with concentration, Charles set out, 23,000 people jumping each fence with him. 'Don't worry about the time, just go for a clear round,' was the instruction. Clear over the first seven fences, there was a huge intake of breath as they approached the final oxer.

– Jenny MacArthur

From left to right: Nick Skelton, Ben Maher, Scott Brash and Peter Charles after a nail-biting jump-off secured a team gold.

London 2012
London 2012
London 2012

Beth Tweddle
Gymnastics

DAY 11 OFFERED Beth Tweddle her last chance to add an Olympic medal to her impressive roll of honour, and for a few dreadful moments it seemed that she had stumbled a step too far.

It was down to the judges. Would they penalise her imperfect dismount from the uneven bars to a degree that would rob the three-times world champion of a place on the podium? Tweddle's mum, Ann, said that she had a 'horrible feeling' in the pit of her stomach. She wasn't the only one. And that explains why this bronze does not seem such a disappointment. Yes, Tweddle possessed the ability to take gold, but for her to have been denied a medal would have been heartbreaking.

Tweddle has been the face of British gymnastics since 2006 and the first of her world titles, but she finished fourth in Beijing and went close to suffering the same fate. 'The step could have cost me,' Tweddle said, 'but do you know what? I don't care. I've got a medal to go home with.'

Tweddle opted not to take any risks with her routine, deciding that her best bet was to perform a less technically challenging option that she knew she could execute to perfection. That perfection eluded her. Her score of 15.916 immediately put her into second place but three more gymnasts had yet to take their turn. Tweddle dropped to third and then had to hope that Gabrielle Douglas would not steal through. Douglas took too few risks and finished last, leaving Tweddle utterly relieved.

'I will sleep well tonight,' the 27-year-old said. 'I haven't slept in three weeks. This has been the longest week of my life. It just finished my career perfectly. I've got every other title. This was the one thing that I was missing. I would have been devastated if I'd walked away with no medal.' Tweddle will not compete at another Olympics, but talk of her retirement is premature.

'I haven't decided exactly what I'm doing,' she said. 'These few weeks have been the most nerve-racking of my life because this was my last chance. I'll soon know if I go back in the gym and my heart's not in it or my body's hurting. I've got to be willing to get up and do the hours, to stay at the top. I don't want to be known as someone who dropped down at the end of her career. I want to walk away from gymnastics on a high.'
– *Alyson Rudd*

Dai Greene

400 metre hurdles

SHOCK, HORROR, something did not go right down at the London love-in in the Athletics Stadium. Dai Greene will have to be content with his world, European and Commonwealth titles after finishing fourth in the 400 metre hurdles final. The Welshman has made a habit of overhauling his opponents in the home straight, but he left himself with a chasm to cross and he could not manage it. Ahead of him the script was ripped up and burnt by the scorched-earth policy of Felix Sanchez.

That it was the 34-year-old Dominican in the lead was as surprising as seeing Greene unable to recapture his best form when it mattered. Sanchez won in a time of 47.63 seconds. Behind him Michael Tinsley of the United States took the silver with Javier Culson, of Puerto Rico, previously unbeaten in 2012, a bemused third.

Greene's time was 48.24 seconds. That was faster than he had run to take the world title in South Korea last year, but the Olympics proved a different proposition. 'Coming into the champs it felt as though I was good enough to get gold – certainly a medal – but the way I felt going into the race I was very fatigued,' he said afterwards.

Greene had collapsed on the track after his semi-final holding his head. Having finished fourth at that stage he was outside the automatic places and cut a sorry figure of fading hope and sepia glory. 'I don't know what happened, I wasn't there. I'm devastated,' he said.

This time he was more rational and knew he had left every drop of energy and passion on the track. However, that semi-final had clearly taken a sledgehammer to his confidence.

Greene has been one of the leading lights in the revival of British athletics over the past Olympic cycle. He won the European, Commonwealth and world titles within a year, but he had knee surgery last winter and, for some reason, has not looked like getting towards the personal best of 47.84 seconds that he set in Paris only a month ago. The frustration for him is that time would have gained him a silver medal. To his credit, he did not go for the knee-jerk reaction and blame the injury.

Of his health and injury issues, he said: 'I would never be able to be world champion if I didn't have those moments.' This is another setback that may ultimately make him stronger.

– Rick Broadbent

Anthony Ogogo and Nicola Adams

Boxing

Above: Anthony Ogogo produced a stellar performance and fought his way into the semi-finals. **Opposite:** The relief and joy etched on her face was evident as Beth Tweddle fulfilled her dreams.

THE DAY ENDED with three medals in the bag and the prospect of more for Team GB, as Anthony Ogogo and Nicola Adams booked their place in the boxing semi-finals, although there was a big disappointment as Savannah Marshall, the women's world champion, was beaten.

Ogogo, the middleweight, produced another excellent performance with a 15–10 points win over Stefan Härtel, of Germany. Nicola Adams confirmed she would at least get a bronze medal at flyweight with a 16–7 points win over Stoyka Petrova, of Bulgaria. Adams, a three-time world silver medal-winner, was expected to win, but having a first bout ten days after the Opening Ceremony was hardly ideal.

Having won the World Championship gold medal in May, Marshall, 21, the middleweight from Hartlepool, was seeded No 1 here and favourite for the gold, but her Olympics ended in tears as she lost 16–12 on points to Marina Volnova, of Kazakhstan, in a nervy, messy affair.

Natasha Jonas was also beaten, but she emerged as a hero after pushing Katie Taylor, of Ireland, to the limit before going down 26–15 on points in a pulsating lightweight quarter-final and possibly the greatest advert for women's boxing you will ever see.

'When you see women's boxing at the highest level and that kind of performance, how can you argue that women aren't just as good as the men?' Jonas said.

– Ron Lewis

Kirani James

400 metres

Kirani James – could he be the successor to Usain Bolt?

SUCCESS AT 400 metres for Grenada's new star may lead to a tilt at 200 metres and a showdown with you-know-who. The night after Usain Bolt, we had Usain Bolt II. And that is not a lazy label, it is one Kirani James has been living with for years. You just wonder what would happen if Bolt I were ever to race Bolt II.

That is maybe an Olympics away. For now, celebrate the new Olympic star in his own right. This is exactly what they will have been doing in the tiny fishing village of Gouyave, in Grenada. They call these parties a 'jump-up'.

Everyone in the community back in Gouyave knows everyone, James said proudly. His father, who is a labourer, will be jumping up as high as any of them.

James is Grenada's first gold medal-winner, he is the island's first medal-winner of any colour at all. And he is only 19. That is the scary bit. In winning the 400 metres, James went under 44 seconds for the first time. Going under 44 seconds is joining the gods. Only nine other men have done it.

Last year he won the World Championships in Daegu, South Korea, and we asked: who is this extraordinary kid? This year, we knew him, we knew his potential, we just didn't know if he was here to command the big stage on a long-term basis. We got his answer.

And it was a performance of Bolt-like supremacy. James is tall, languid, powerful and genetically ideal. The quarter-mile is a test of speed endurance, but James does not seem to tire. He had caught the field by the last 100 metres, but where they were plateauing, hanging on for all they could, James powered on.

James was asked when he would start to double up, as he did as a junior, and run the 200 metres, too. 'That's in the future,' he said, a glint in his eye. 'For now it's the 400 metres. The 200 metres is a way too talented field. You have to respect them.' Respectful as that may be, that 'future' he mentioned sounds spectacular.

But all that is for the future. The Olympics tell us so much about superpowers and sporting development systems and yet here we have the boy from nowhere who has the world completely and utterly at his feet.

– Owen Slot

Day 11 Round Up

BASKETBALL
Great Britain finally recorded their first victory in the 2012 Olympics, defeating China by 90–58, a result that means they finished ninth in a 12-team field.

CANOEING
Tim Brabants, Britain's defending Olympic champion, scraped into the final of the men's canoe sprint.

In other events, Jess Walker, Rachel Cawthorn, Angela Hannah and Louisa Sawers made it through to the final of the K4 500 metres, however, in the C1 1,000 metres, Richard Jefferies failed to make it through to the final.

SAILING
Tom Slingsby won Australia's second gold medal with victory in the Laser sailing event. Slingsby had won the three races before the medal race, which meant that he needed only to stop Pavlos Kontides from being in the top four to win gold. Kontides's silver was a first Olympic medal for Cyprus.

HANDBALL
The adventure is over, but Team GB saved their best to last in a 41–24 loss to Iceland. The team produced their best display in the first half to match the Scandinavians, but fell away.

SHOOTING
Britain's hopes of adding to Peter Wilson's gold medal ended when Ed Ling failed to make the final of the men's trap. The 29-year-old from Somerset was well placed after the first three rounds, scoring 72 out of 75, and started with a perfect 25. But his final round of 21 left him well outside the top six who qualified for the final.

Wilson followed James Huckle and Jonathan Hammond out of the Games, the Britain pair failing to make the final of the 50 metres rifle three positions.

WEIGHTLIFTING
China won eight weightlifting gold medals at the Beijing Games four years ago and struck gold again in the opening event as Wang Mingjuan won the under-48kg women's event.

MEDAL TABLE

	Gold	Silver	Bronze	T
1. CHINA	31	19	14	64
2. USA	29	15	19	63
3. GREAT BRITAIN	18	11	11	40
4. SOUTH KOREA	11	5	6	22
5. FRANCE	8	9	9	26

GYMNASTICS: WOMEN'S UNEVEN BARS FINAL

Gold RUS

16.133

Silver CHN

15.933

Bronze GBR

15.916

07.08.12
London 2012 Olympic Games
Day 12

Medals won by Team GB
Gold 4
Silver 2
Bronze 2

12

Chris Hoy
Keirin

Day 12 of London 2012 will be remembered by Chris Hoy as the day on which he retired from Olympic competition in spectacular style. He finished his last race dominant still, the winner of six golds, and no doubt the rest of the world breathing a sigh of relief.

Hoy was racing five men, but so dominant has his grip been on this competition that there was only one man in the field who even had a proper go at beating him. With a lap to go, though, he had not looked quite so smooth. As the riders hit the bell, even at speeds of 70kmph, they glanced left for information from their coach; that was when Hoy saw his man, Jan van Eijden, gesticulating furiously at him. Van Eijden could see the nightmare scenario unfolding. He saw Hoy at the front, dominating, but what he calls 'feathering the throttle'. In other words, Hoy was not giving it full gas and Van Eijden could see the German, Max Levy, moving up, waiting to attack.

Hoy, at this stage, was in a classic position to lose the race. But the reason Hoy now has more gold medals than other Olympians is because these are the moments where he is different to normal mortals, these are the moments when he thrives.

In his trail were Van Velthooven, the Kiwi, and three others who were happy just to follow his wheel. They did not challenge him, they were not prepared to risk their hand at a gamble they had already concluded would most likely fail. Levy, though, was the exception. 'I was the only one who had the heart to attack,' he said. 'I wanted to try.' He slid up alongside Hoy, and as they entered the bend, his front wheel had edged ahead.

That was when Hoy responded like the multi-champion, the guy who keeps a calm hand on victory when it is slipping away. He knew he had to hold the black line on the bend; if he did, Levy would be defeated on the outside.

What happened next belongs to many people. Hoy credits the crowd. Just when he needed help, he said, 'You feel its big hand pushing you along the track.' Levy tried to take the black line but could not squeeze in. Hoy held it, led into the straight and was victorious.

It was a wonderful, emotional way to end it. The race told a great story; of a great British Olympian still dominant, even at the last.
– Owen Slot

Laura Trott
Omnium

JUST BEFORE Hoy's extraordinary finale to his career, another Team GB cyclist lit up the Velodrome with a performance that suggests a new star is rising.

Jessica Ennis is not the only multi-tasking British bright spark in the Olympic Village. In the diminutive form of Laura Trott, cycling has its own beaming vision of versatility, who, at the age of 20, already has two Olympic gold medals to her name after clinching a dramatic victory in the omnium to follow the team pursuit success.

To put that into context, Sir Chris Hoy won his first gold medal in Athens at 28, Victoria Pendleton the first of her two in Beijing at 27. Trott is going to be around for a while and she has only just started.

Across the two days and six events of the omnium, Trott was always in contention. She finished first in two of the first five events and was second in the 3,000 metres individual pursuit behind Sarah Hammer, of the United States, who moved into first place ahead of Trott. The British rider then provided the tongs to her rival's hammer in a combative scratch race, at the end of which Trott remained two points behind going into the final race, the 500-metre time trial.

The omnium awards one point to the winner of each event, the overall winner being the rider with the fewest points so Trott, riding head-to-head with Hammer, had to finish three clear places ahead.

This is a rider who used to vomit before races because of a stomach condition, but her focus never wavered. Standing 5ft nothing and weighing 8st wet through, her long pigtails tucked into her helmet, Trott's appearance belies the power she transmits through the pedals and she clearly possesses a formidable competitive spirit.

Urged on by the thunderous volume of the Velodrome crowd, she finished precisely three places ahead of Hammer, precisely according to plan. With an average speed of 51kmph over two frenetic laps, she finished with the best time, 35.110 seconds. Hammer, who slipped away badly in the final lap, finished fourth, and the gold medal was Trott's by a single, precious point.

Home advantage, once again, in its most elemental form. 'My legs were killing me,' she said. 'But the crowd really drove me on, I'd never have done it without them.'

Her older sister, Emma, stands to benefit from Laura's success, as the younger sibling promised to buy her a car if she won both gold medals. The sisters were introduced to cycling at their local track in Welwyn Garden City when their mother wanted to lose weight. 'I really didn't like it at first, it was always cold and I just didn't enjoy it,' she said. 'But then I won a couple of races, I liked the feeling and after that I didn't want to not win.'

With performances like this, Trott looks likely to experience that feeling again many times as a long and potentially glorious career stretches out ahead of her.

– *John Westerby*

Laura Trott secured her second gold medal after a last push on the pedals.

Equestrian team
Dressage

For the British equestrian team, these Games will be remembered as the ones in which they broke an Olympic medal drought. Less than 24 hours after their showjumpers won an historic gold, the dressage team – led by Carl Hester – became Olympic champions. Scintillating performances from all three riders in the grand prix special, the final round of the team event, relegated Germany to silver and the Netherlands to bronze.

It is the first time in the 100-year history of the sport that Britain have won an Olympic dressage medal – let alone a gold.

For Charlotte Dujardin, 27, who rode her first grand prix only last year, it was a massive leap to the top of the sport. Riding Valegro, a ten-year-old owned jointly by Hester and Roly Luard, she gained the highest score of the day, 83.286 per cent, an Olympic record.

Hester, 45, her mentor and the architect of the team's success, had paved the way for the gold medal with a score of 80.540 per cent on his and Sasha Stewart's Uthopia. Laura Bechtolsheimer, 27, followed with a 77.873 per cent on her triple world silver medal-winner, Mistral Hojris.

It was then up to Dujardin, put in the third spot by Hester 'because she thrives on pressure', to repeat the winning performance she delivered in the grand prix.

'I was nervous going in,' Dujardin said. 'I wanted that gold medal so badly and I didn't want to mess up. I'm just so lucky to be riding Valegro. He's the horse of a lifetime, he finds it all so easy.'

Hester not only trained his own horse, but also coached Dujardin and her horse. Hester's dual role began when Dujardin arrived at his Gloucestershire yard five years ago for a lesson and 'never left'. Hester recognised 'a huge talent' and offered her Valegro. 'I thought she could take him through novice classes and I would get him back when he became international,' Hester said.

So successful was the partnership – they won at every novice level – that Hester allowed her to keep the ride. Hester was so determined to nurture Dujardin in time for London that he neglected his own preparation. 'I came to London with a slight lack of confidence as a result,' he said.

No one would have guessed that from his performance. Uthopia was a model of obedience, the over-exuberance of his grand prix test giving way to a stunning display in which he went into the lead – and temporarily held the Olympic record.

Bechtolsheimer then produced an assured test on Mistral Hojris, 17. She revealed that far from feeling excluded from the Hester/Dujardin dynamic, she feels a part of it. 'I've known Carl since I was 10 when he worked for my father,' she said. Her father, Wilfried Bechtolsheimer, a member of the Britain team at the 1995 European Championships, was the first to congratulate the team after Dujardin's winning test.

'We can't believe it – first medal ever and the gold,' he said. 'To have something like this is so special – will it ever happen again?'

– *Jenny MacArthur*

Alistair and Jonny Brownlee
Triathlon

I N A DAY WHEN medals seemed to shower down on Team GB, two were awarded in one event, to brothers standing side by side on the podium.

There was a moment in this dramatic triathlon when Jonny Brownlee glanced at the board that indicated a 15-second penalty for one competitor. 'I saw No 31 had a penalty and thought, "Alistair, what an idiot,"' Jonny said. 'Then I looked down and realised it was me.'

This was an event that had everything. As an estimated 200,000 gathered around Hyde Park,

Buckingham Palace and Wellington Arch while millions more watched at home, it may have been the day triathlon came of age in Britain.

The sport has two new heroes for the mainstream, a couple of nice lads from Yorkshire whose profile has just soared. Alistair and Jonny Brownlee live together, train together – and now they have stood on a podium together in a touching moment of history. No Briton had won an Olympic medal in triathlon before and now Alistair had gold, Jonny bronze.

In their success also came the revelation of what triathlon is about: the demands, the tactics, the test of mind and body and the punishment it inflicts. Jonny drove himself so close to exhaustion that the medal ceremony had to be delayed for almost an hour so that he could receive medical treatment. The younger Brownlee had to be covered in wet towels and ice, then carried on a wheelchair to a medical room where he was sick. Glucose and water were administered, but it took a long time before he could stand on his feet.

It was not much easier for Alistair either. The 2011 world champion may have started as favourite, but there was nothing routine about his victory. Alistair ripped his Achilles tendon in late January. He could not run for several months, yet here he sprinted at an extraordinary speed. To run straight off the bike, thigh muscles full of lactic acid, is disorientating for the legs. But the first kilometre was covered at 28-minute pace for 10 kilometres. Consider that Mo Farah won gold with a time of 27 minutes 30 seconds – and that was without swimming 1.5 kilometres through the Serpentine and then cycling for 43 kilometres around London's streets at breakneck speed.

The brothers in arms made history as they became the first British medal winners in the Olympic triathlon event.

Alistair completed his 10 kilometres in 29:07, a second slower than Chris Thompson, Farah's GB team-mate, had. His time would have been quicker still if he had not slowed for the final 100 metres to grab a Union Jack from a spectator and wrap it around his shoulders in a wonderful moment of exhausted showboating. A sprint became a jog and then a walk as he crossed the line 11 seconds ahead of Javier Gómez, the Spaniard, and 20 seconds ahead of his brother.

Coming out of the swim in the first six, the brothers had been intent on forming a breakaway group on the bike. But Jonny was a little too eager. He leapt onto his bike while standing inside the transition area, which prompted the penalty.

Alistair sought to keep his little brother's spirits high but Jonny fretted. Wisely ignoring advice from the coaches to take the penalty immediately he came off the bike, Jonny stayed with Alistair and Gómez for as long as possible on the run before being dropped on the third lap of four. He had built enough of a lead over two Frenchmen to stand in the penalty box and still return in the bronze-medal position for the final lap. Might he have won silver without his mistake? 'We'll never know but I don't think it changed the race,' he said.

Two years ago Alistair had collapsed in a Hyde Park triathlon and is still unable to recall what happened. Here he had plenty of glorious memories, not least discovering that the Brownlees were briefly ranked 36th in the medals table.

Alistair, unpersuaded by suggestions that he should race Farah, will seek to defend his title in Rio. But, staring out over Hyde Park, he acknowledged: 'It may never get better than this.' – *Matt Dickinson*

Victoria Pendleton
Individual sprint

AFTER THE UPS and downs of her Games in London, one British athlete was excited to finish her last event with a silver medal to mark the end of a glittering Olympic career.

Steve Redgrave once told the world to shoot him if he went near a boat. Then he returned, famously, for that fifth Olympic gold. After the race Victoria Pendleton said that she would never race a bike again 'if you paid me a million, billion pounds'. You can stake your life that this Olympic hero will be true to her word.

After two Olympic golds and nine world titles, Pendleton's career has concluded and it was relief that overwhelmed her, not sadness that her finale ended with defeat and a silver medal. No more fighting battles, especially with herself; no more wondering why she puts herself through the agonies; no more visits to the sport's shrink.

The Velodrome has been the most intense arena at these Olympics, and the intensity reached a new fever pitch as Pendleton faced her arch rival, Anna Meares. Controversy struck in the first race. As Meares came thundering round the outside into the final straight, she threw out an elbow. There was little contact but Pendleton moved across, fatefully. The photo-finish showed Pendleton to have won by a thousandth of a second, by the width of a tyre, but she was relegated on inquiry for straying outside the sprinter's line.

The psychological blow was huge. And what Pendleton did not know was that Meares had hatched a cunning plan for race two. As Pendleton stayed tight to her rival's wheel on the first lap, Meares slowed to a crawl and then to a halt on the banking, balanced on pedals. Pendleton had no option than to come past. Suddenly she was in the wrong place. As Pendleton led from the front with no conviction, Meares took her easily in the sprint.

One gold, one silver and a disqualification from Pendleton's final Games was more than enough to satisfy her. 'I won't ever don a skinsuit again,' she said, 'and I won't miss it. I've been racing since 1989. I haven't missed a season. Cycling fell in my lap. It wasn't a dream or an ambition. It was me having something in common with my dad and I happened to be quite good at it.' With tears in her eyes, Pendleton departed as one of the greats.
– Matt Dickinson

Going out on a high – Victoria Pendleton waved goodbye to competitive cycling with a silver medal.

Nick Dempsey

Windsurfing

At the National Sailing Academy, Nick Dempsey, Britain's silver surfer, was carried up the slipway by six team-mates, standing on his surfboard with the Union Jack over his shoulders. It was as if he had won gold, but Dempsey had done something far more important. By finishing second he had exorcised the demons of Beijing.

Four years ago Dempsey suffered agony in the medal race on the waters off Qingdao, slipping from a possible gold medal to no medal in the final 300 metres. To rub it in, Sarah Ayton, his fiancée, now wife, won a gold medal in the Yngling on the same day. Despite becoming world champion a year later, he has spent four long years waiting for another chance for an Olympic medal.

That it was only a silver did not matter to Dempsey. Dorian van Rijsselberge, from the Netherlands, had sailed a near perfect regatta and had the gold sewn up with two races to go. Dempsey needed to finish in the top six to guarantee the silver, which he did by clinging to Van Rijsselberge's wake to cross the line third.

'I am just massively relieved. I was desperate to finish second. Third would have been a disaster and fourth, well I don't know what I would have done.' Dempsey, 31, said.

As cheers rang out from the 5,000-strong crowd gathered on the Nothe Gardens, Dempsey hitched a lift on a support boat before diving into the sea, swimming to shore and clambering up the rocks to give his sons Thomas, 3, and Oscar, 5 months, a hug and a kiss. Thomas, who has a new sparkly medal to show off at nursery school, asked: 'Have you finished work now, Daddy?' Dempsey told him he had finished for the week.

This was Dempsey's fourth Olympics and his best result. This could be the last time that windsurfing is in the Olympics. It has provisionally been dropped for the 2016 Games in favour of kite-surfing. Dempsey denied that an upheld decision would mean the end of his Olympic career. 'It's a moment for reflection but I'm pretty sure it's not the end of the road,' he said. The prospect of competing with his wife in the new mixed multihull event for 2016 was rejected, but Dempsey suggested he may give kite-surfing a go. 'I haven't tried it yet, but I have ordered some kites,' he said.
– *Patrick Kidd*

Robbie Grabarz

High jump

LOTTERY FUNDING loser Robbie Grabarz won a bronze medal as the evening drew in at the Olympic Stadium and then, having jumped one bar, probably headed for another. The maverick of the British team said that he fancied a party in the Olympic Village.

Ivan Ukhov certainly looked up for a party. The hirsute Russian won the gold medal with a jump of 2.38 metres. Meanwhile, in second place with a leap of 2.33 was Eric Kynard, of the United States.

Grabarz may be more eccentric than all the other athletes. He said he was deservedly kicked off the funding programme last year and his coach gave him a strongly worded ultimatum to stop wasting their time. The 24-year-old from Enfield went to his local pub and spent a couple of days soul-searching. He contemplated going into the classic car industry, but then decided: 'How great is this life? I turn up to a track, mess around for a couple of hours, travel the world, see a lot of things and get to wear a tracksuit all the time.'

It is hard not to warm to someone so seemingly nonchalant about his Olympic appearance. It was less than a year ago when he was still thinking about whether to bother with this sport lark. He had already dropped out of Loughborough University, the renowned base for sporting hopefuls, because he said all anyone ever did was talk about sport. That was six weeks in. A few years on and he has an Olympic medal.

His only regret was that he should have claimed silver. 'I was slightly miffed, because I should have jumped higher than that and should have got one better medal,' he said. 'But, I got a bronze medal and it's incredible, slightly surreal.'

Before the Olympics, Grabarz suggested that it would be good fun to drag Ukhov out for a night. Often, when on the circuit, Grabarz wanders out into foreign fields to sink a couple of beers. Now he may have found his match in more ways than one.
– Rick Broadbent

Grabarz in a sober moment before securing a silver medal.

Men's team
Hockey

A FURIOUS ROW overshadowed Great Britain's celebrations after they qualified for their first Olympic semi-final since 1988. Spain's coach all but accused the umpires of favouritism as the home team held on grimly for a dramatic 1–1 draw at the Riverbank Arena.

Resolutely defending against a furious onslaught by the 2008 Beijing silver medal-winners in a nerve-racking final quarter, two penalty corners awarded to Spain in the last three minutes were overturned by the umpires.

Dani Martín, the coach, could scarcely contain his fury at the press conference. 'It simply cannot happen that officials change decisions when they're surrounded by [GB] players,' he said. 'There are clear favourites here among some teams and if the president of the International Hockey Federation [FIH] doesn't give an explanation there will be consequences.'

Jason Lee, the Britain head coach, said he thought the umpires made the decisions independently and showed good clarity of thought under pressure, before saying: 'It's a research fact that officials in any sport go with the pressure quite often, and there was certainly a lot of pressure on them. There are 50–50 decisions and under pressure it's hard for the umpires. It's not life and death out there but it is really important.'

What Leandro Negre, the FIH president and a Spaniard, will make of the controversy remains to be seen, but in the frenzied finish when they forced four penalty corners in the last four minutes, Spain have every reason to believe they might just have broken British hearts.

With Britain needing only a draw to qualify, it sets up a semi-final with the Netherlands, gold medal-winners in 1996 and 2000, while Australia's crushing 7–0 victory over Pakistan meant they finish top of the group and go into a contest in the last four against Germany, the Olympic champions.

Not since the golden days of Seoul in 1988 have a Britain team been under so much pressure to deliver. The last time they beat Spain in a leading competition was at the Champions Trophy in 1987, when they won 5–1.

– Cathy Harris

Phillips Idowu
Triple jump

WHILE GRABARZ was jumping for joy in the Olympic Stadium, British team-mate Phillips Idowu ended up far from the winners' podium.

After the spat, the polish. That was the plan, but Phillips Idowu failed to put a troubled build-up behind him and so his Olympic career came to a sad and sometimes silly end.

The 2009 world champion triple jumper had been accused of turning his back on the Great Britain team by Charles van Commenee, the head coach, as a protracted injury saga was played out to the sound of denials, half-truths and mudslinging.

On the eve of the Games, Van Commenee dubbed Idowu 'the invisible man', blamed him for breaking off communications with his coach and even claimed he had no idea if and when he would turn up. He did, but it was clear that all the talk of injuries was well founded. Idowu has had a trapped nerve, causing pain in his leg, knee and hip.

The 2008 silver medal-winner jumped only 16.53 metres and was fourteenth in the qualifying competition. He missed the cut.

Idowu missed the Olympic trials in July and Van Commenee admitted the reason was injury. When Idowu pitched up on a boat on the Thames, he fudged the issue, saying that he had never said he was injured. Days later, the Hackney hero pulled out of the Aviva London Grand Prix, citing hip pain as the problem.

In desperate straits, he chose to stay in London and work with a physiotherapist instead of going to the training camp in Portugal. That might have been the end of it, but for Idowu and Van Commenee not speaking and so the Dutchman had no firm idea of his injury. Then the BOA got involved, asking to see his medical records. As spat turned into farce, Idowu's camp said they were furious with the BOA for making public demands.

In the circumstances it would have been a huge shock if Idowu had turned up in the sort of shape that would have threatened the podium. 'I don't think you've seen the best of me,' he insisted, but he is 33. Whatever the rights and wrongs of an unseemly saga, it is hard not to feel some sympathy for a man who has been a big performer for Britain over the years.

– Rick Broadbent

Liu Xiang

110 metre hurdles

After all his hard work at recovering his form, Liu Xiang's Olympic dreams were dashed at the first hurdle.

THE MAN WHO broke a billion hearts fell at the first hurdle for the second Olympics in a row. Liu Xiang crashed into the barrier during his heat of the 110 metres hurdles and fell to the track in pain and despair. As the crowd gasped, Liu was left to consider that he had been unable to clear a single obstacle in two Olympic Games.

Four years ago Liu was the face of the Games, China's Jessica Ennis. The State limited his phone calls so that he could train harder. Then he turned up to the Beijing Olympics nursing an Achilles injury. He tried to compete, but limped away from the Bird's Nest before his heat.

Fast forward and this was to be his catharsis. But after four years of rebuilding himself he crashed into the first barrier in his heat. His team leader, Feng Shuyong, said he had ruptured the same Achilles when he tried to lift off. Nevertheless, Liu picked himself up and hopped on one leg all the way down the side of the straight, before leaning against the final hurdle.

'Seeing him hopping to the line shows the true spirit of the Olympics,' Feng said. 'He was determined to get to the end.'

It is one of those sights that only the Olympics throws up. Liu has an Olympic gold from 2004 and broke the world record in 2006, but he would have traded both to be fit in Beijing. Now, after missing out on gold at last year's World Championships when he was accidentally hauled back by Dayron Robles, his misfortune continues.

It was impossible not to feel his pain. Andy Turner, the Briton who won the heat, helped Liu off the track. 'I looked slightly to my left about halfway and didn't see Liu and was surprised, thinking, "What's going on?" It's not often you get to beat Liu Xiang. I didn't realise he had stopped. It was horrible seeing him limp off so you have to go and help people. He's a nice guy and I wouldn't wish that on my worst enemy.'
– Rick Broadbent

Day 12 Round Up

GYMNASTICS

Deng Linlin won her first individual Olympic gold medal on the balance beam on the final day of gymnastics at the North Greenwich Arena. Alexandra Raisman, of the US, took bronze after an appeal placed her above Catalina Ponor, the 2004 triple gold medal-winner, from Romania. Raisman also took gold on the floor, with Ponor the silver and Aliya Mustafina, of Russia, the bronze.

China finished top of the medal table after winning two more golds. Feng Zhe was first in the parallel bars, ahead of Marcel Nguyen, of Germany, and Hamilton Sabot, of France.

Epke Zonderland, of the Netherlands, won an epic horizontal bar final, beating Fabian Hambüchen, of Germany, and Zou Kai, of China.

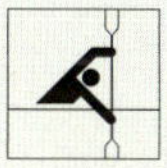

CANOEING

Rachel Cawthorn booked her place in the final of the women's sprint kayak. The 23-year-old won her heat in the K1 500 metres impressively and then came second in her semi-final. However, there was disappointment for Louisa Sawers, 24, and Abigail Edmonds, 21, who failed to reach the final of the women's double kayak.

SYNCHRONISED SWIMMING

Natalia Ishchenko and Svetlana Romashina helped Russia to keep a stranglehold on synchronised swimming with gold in the duet on 98.900 after the free routine, for a total of 197.100 points after three days of competition. The silver went to Ona Carbonell Ballestero and Andrea Fuentes Fache, of Spain, and the bronze to Xuechen Huang and Ou Liu, of China.

Jenna Randall and Olivia Federici, the Great Britain pair, finished ninth on 177.270 points as the first British synchronised swimmers to make an Olympic final since 1992.

TABLE TENNIS

China are one gold medal away from a second successive clean sweep after their women marched to a 3–0 victory over a young Japan team.

FOOTBALL

Mexico reached the final of the men's tournament for the first time in their history after coming from behind to defeat Japan 3–1.

MEDAL TABLE

				T
1. CHINA	34	21	18	73
2. USA	30	19	21	70
3. GREAT BRITAIN	22	13	13	48
4. SOUTH KOREA	12	5	6	23
5. RUSSIA	10	18	20	48

TRIATHLON: MEN

Gold GBR

1:46:25

Silver ESP

1:46:36

Bronze GBR

1:46.56

CLARKE

08.08.12
London 2012 Olympic Games
Day 13

Medals won by Team GB
Gold 0
Silver 0
Bronze 0

13

Women's team
Hockey

In a valiantly fought semi-final, Argentina dealt a deadly blow to Britain's gold-medal hopes.

HAVING FOUGHT a valiant battle into the semi-finals, Argentina crushed the dreams of Great Britain's women's hockey team of playing for the gold medal when they completely outclassed the home team to show why they are the world champions, winning 2–1 at the Riverbank Arena.

Leading 2–0 at half-time, Argentina held firm as Britain mounted a determined late challenge, but after chasing hard for most of the match, they gave themselves far too much to do.

Argentina will meet the Netherlands, the reigning champions, who saw off New Zealand in a tense shoot-out after the sides were level at 2–2 after extra time, in the final with Britain taking on the Black Sticks in the play-off for the bronze.

There was no more poignant moment in defeat than watching Kate Walsh sink to her knees at the final whistle. The captain has earned widespread praise for her bravery, returning to the action five days after having surgery to insert a titanium plate in her broken jaw. Playing with a protective mask, the 32-year-old turned in a typically resolute display at the back, cajoling her players and never shirking a tackle. No one deserves to play for a medal more than she does.

It has been a long wait for Britain, who won their solitary Olympic medal when they collected bronze in Barcelona in 1992 and last contested the medal rounds at the Atlanta Games in 1996.

After successive defeats, it was going to take an extraordinary performance to beat Argentina and they made the worst possible start when Noel Barrionuevo drilled in a sixth-minute penalty corner. In a woeful first half, the home team struggled to string three passes together and rarely threatened their opponents' goal. Four minutes before the interval, Aymar set up her side's second goal. Pushing forward desperately after the restart, Britain piled on the pressure without carving out many clear-cut chances. Helen Richardson had the best opportunity in the 55th minute but, with the goal gaping, her weak effort missed the target.

However, she atoned for the error six minutes from time, sending in the perfect cross for Alex Danson to deflect in. Roared on by the crowd, Britain threw everything at Argentina in a thrilling finale but it was too little, too late.
– *Cathy Harris*

'I can't believe I came fourth in the Olympic Games. I didn't expect to make the finals.' Lawrence Clarke

Lawrence Clarke

110 metre hurdles

LAWRENCE CLARKE, heir to the Baronetcy of Clarke of Dunham Lodge, and inspired by the memory of Lord Burghley, the Olympic aristocrat, proved that he is the toff of the track on Day 13.

The 22-year-old was going to the Olympics for the experience, but he almost got a medal, finishing fourth in the men's 110 metres hurdles, one of the most competitive of all events in the track and field programme.

Aries Merritt, the in-form American, won the title in a personal best of 12.92 seconds, making him the joint sixth-fastest man in history. Jason Richardson, the world champion, was second in 13.04 seconds with Hansle Parchment, of Jamaica, third in a national record of 13.12 seconds.

'I can't believe I came fourth in the Olympic Games,' Clarke said. 'I didn't expect to make the final and treated the semi as the final. I ran a personal best, which was a dream come true, I then had a waiting game to see if I was in the final. 'The last four years have been an amazing journey. Malcolm [Arnold, his coach] has taken me from running 15.3 seconds to running 13.3 tonight. I can't thank him enough.'

Clarke's joy introduces an interesting character to the British public. If he was unfazed by the prospect of taking on the best in front of 80,000 people at the age of only 22, it may have come from the fact he climbed Mont Blanc at the age of 13.

His great-grandmother was Elfrida Roosevelt, so he is first cousin, four times removed, from Theodore Roosevelt, 26th President of the United States and second cousin, four times removed, from Franklin Delano Roosevelt, the 32nd President. Bucking the trend for athletes to pick recent runners as heroes, he cites Lord David Burghley, the Olympic athlete and sixth Marquess of Exeter, indelibly portrayed by Nigel Havers in *Chariots of Fire*.

Clarke has a bronze medal from the Commonwealth Games but should not dwell on how close he was to winning the same colour on the greatest stage. This was some achievement, even if it was helped by Cuba's defending champion, Dayron Robles, not finishing the race after pulling up injured, more collateral damage of the most unpredictable of events.

– Rick Broadbent

Allyson Felix
200 metres

IF ATHLETICS were a competition for grace and beauty on the move, then Allyson Felix would not have won her first Olympic individual gold medal here in the Olympic Stadium on Day 13. It would have been her third. She is still only 26, yet it seems that for a lifetime she has been gliding stylishly around Olympic tracks.

She draped her stars and stripes around her shoulders and set off on a victory lap with a beam across her face that reflected the wait.

Athletics is a sport forever in search of new heroes and when Felix first appeared on the horizon she was fresh, tiny and she seemed to float. Anyone who watched her saw it, the gliding, a kind of female Carl Lewis whose feet barely brushed the floor. And aged 18, there she was at the Athens Games, in the final of the 200 metres. She won silver, behind Veronica Campbell-Brown of Jamaica. You just wondered what would happen when she came of age.

She won gold in the World Championships in Helsinki. And then she did it again in 2007, and then again in 2009. Three world titles in succession; the missing link was the Olympic equivalent. In Berlin in 2009, as she cherished her third world gold, she turned to Campbell-Brown, whom she had beaten into silver, and told her: 'I would love to trade my three World Championships for your Olympic gold.' By then, Campbell-Brown had collected a second.

In Beijing, Campbell-Brown had lined up again in a lane next to Felix, had taken out a firm lead and defended it all the way to the line. That was when doubters started to wonder: would Felix ever get her just deserts?

Here she did not allow Campbell-Brown a lead to defend. Here she maintained her stride all the way to the line, gliding to Olympic victory at last.

– *Owen Slot*

At long last, Allyson Felix achieved the Olympic gold that had been eluding her.

Day 13 Round Up

TABLE TENNIS
China won gold in the men's team event, beating South Korea and adding to their triumphs in the individual events and the women's team competition.

BASKETBALL
France showed their fighting spirit as they exited at the quarter-final stage, losing 66–59 to Spain, who advance to meet Russia in the last four.

Russia dramatically beat Lithuania 83–74, leaving David Blatt with a bloody nose after an overexuberant celebration with his coaching staff.

VOLLEYBALL
The United States, the defending champions, relinquished their title when they were beaten in straight sets by Italy in their quarter-final at Earls Court, losing 28–26, 25–20, 25–20.

In the semi-finals, Italy, the No 6 seeds, will take on Brazil, who claimed the silver medal in Beijing four years ago, after they comfortably beat Argentina 3–0.

HANDBALL
Hungary dramatically progressed to the semi-finals after defeating Iceland, silver medal-winners in Beijing, 34–33 in a double extra-time thriller.

HOCKEY
The women's hockey teams of New Zealand and the Netherlands made history, in the first Olympic penalty shoot-out. The Netherlands won through to the final after winning the shoot-out 3–1.

ATHLETICS
The first woman to compete on the Olympic track for Saudi Arabia took a giant leap forward for her nation, and received a standing ovation from the London crowd. Sarah Attar was last in her 800 metres heat, finishing more than a minute and a half slower than the next athlete, but her run will be quick to take a place in women's history.

MEDAL TABLE

				T
1. CHINA	36	22	19	77
2. USA	34	22	25	81
3. GREAT BRITAIN	22	13	13	48
4. SOUTH KOREA	12	7	6	25
5. RUSSIA	11	19	22	52

TOP NATIONS: ATHLETICS MEDALS IN NUMBERS

USA

20

(5G 8S 7B)

RUS

9

(3G 2S 4B)

GBR

5

(3G 1S 1B)

London 2012
adidas

09.08.12
London 2012 Olympic Games
Day 14

Medals won by Team GB
Gold 3
Silver 0
Bronze 1

14

Jade Jones
Taekwondo

DAY 14 WAS ladies' day, or a day of firsts, when the women took golds in events that had eluded Great Britain in the past.

Jade Jones claimed her slice of British Olympic history as she defeated Hou Yuzhuo, the former double world champion from China, in the under-57kg final to become the first Briton to claim an Olympic gold in taekwondo. Sarah Stevenson, 29, was the last woman to claim a taekwondo medal, bronze in Beijing four years ago.

Her team-mate, Martin Stamper, had played his part in rousing the audience but he lost his semi-final against Rohullah Nikpah, of Afghanistan, in the under-68kg category.

But the final glory was for the Great Britain taekwondo team's baby. Just being in an Olympic final at the age of 19 was a momentous achievement for Jones, after she beat Li-Cheng Tseng, from Chinese Taipei, the world No 1, in the semi-finals.

It was reflected by the cheers that rang down around the ExCel Centre. Up in the darkness of the stands, was a horde of family and friends dissolving with emotion at an occasion that went beyond the confines of London and the Olympics.

Jones has been on an extraordinary journey that comes courtesy of the town of Flint, whose residents were prepared to put their hands in their pockets to help one of their youngsters add her name to the roster of Olympians. Two years ago, Jones needed £1,600 to finance a trip to compete in the Youth Olympic Games in Singapore. Her family were doing their best but overseas flights and hotels were a stretch too far – until Flint came to her aid with a whip-round. Jones repaid their faith then with gold – and this time it was gold again for Flint's famous child.

'You want to see Flint,' said Gary Jones, Jade's father. 'They have done everything for my daughter. They have put flags out, pictures, and the pubs are choc-a-bloc. She has brought Flint together.' And all for the youngster with attitude who was taken to a taekwondo class at the age of seven by her grandfather to burn off her temper.

A fiercely gruelling day of combat with the world's best: four bouts in a single day, culminated in the Olympic final and a chance of a gold medal. It was not a day to forget for Jones – or the good people of Flint.

– *Kevin Eason*

Nicola Adams
Boxing

The stuff that dreams are made of. Nicola Adams celebrates a fairytale ending to her first Olympics.

NEXT IN LINE to make history was Nicola Adams; not only was she the first British woman to take Olympic gold in boxing, but she was the first to win in Olympic women's boxing.

The new champion celebrated with a big smile, an arm in the air and a little Ali Shuffle. 'That's now the Nicki Shuffle,' she said.

Adams had been simply brilliant, dancing her way through a tricky draw to win flyweight gold with ease, with a punch-perfect display in the final to beat Ren Cancan, of China, 16–7 on points.

'It's like a fairytale,' she said. 'I dreamed of this since I was 12 years old. I watched videos of Muhammad Ali and Sugar Ray Leonard getting their gold medals and now I've got mine.' There were no tears. 'I was holding them back,' Adams said. This was the perfect conclusion to the inaugural women's tournament.

This week some have shrunk when faced with the cauldron of noise in the ExCel Olympic boxing arena. Adams, though, has shone, making her way into the final with ease, despite potentially tricky encounters against Stoyka Petrova, of Bulgaria, and Mary Kom, of India. And the way she handled the final was just stunning.

'I was confident going for the win,' Adams said. 'I have been confident all week and I knew I could beat her this time. When I got into the ring, I could hear the fans chanting my name and I thought "bloody hell".' Ren started the faster, but Adams bided her time and landed cleanly with the straight right, building up a 4–2 lead at the end of the first round. But Adams's big moment came halfway through the second round, as a left jab knocked Ren on her heels and a right put her on her back. There was no way back from that for Ren. After two of the four rounds, she trailed 9–4 and had to chase the bout, while Adams could box on the back foot Adams picked her punches beautifully, extending her lead to 14–5.

Adams will now find herself the sport's poster girl in Britain, not only a pioneer but an idol. 'Hearing kids say they want to be boxers like me is amazing,' she said. 'It's amazing to think I could get them into boxing and they want to achieve what I've done. I was really trying to fight back the tears when I was standing on the podium. I was thinking it's here, I've done it. I don't think I will ever stop smiling.'
– Ron Lewis

‘Hearing kids say they want to be boxers like me is amazing. It’s amazing to think they want to achieve what I’ve done.’

Charlotte Dujardin

Dressage

ANOTHER GREAT young hope dazzled the crowd at Greenwich Park as she took gold for Team GB. The wait for the score was almost unbearable and when it came – 90.089 per cent – the roar from the 23,000-strong crowd thronging the dressage arena at Greenwich Park all but drowned out the announcement.

Charlotte Dujardin, 27, sensationally brought the curtain down on equestrian events, breaking the Olympic record to add the individual dressage gold medal to the team gold already won.

Her team-mate Laura Bechtolsheimer took the individual bronze on Mistral Hojris, behind Adelinde Cornelissen, of the Netherlands, to bring the total number of equestrian medals won in London to a record three gold, one silver and a bronze. Dujardin, who rode a spellbinding test on Valegro in the Freestyle to Music category – much of it to 'Land of Hope and Glory' – becomes only the second British rider after the eventer Richard Meade to win double gold.

'He was brilliant. He went out there and gave his all – he's the horse of a lifetime and he means the world to me.'

It is a phenomenal achievement. Dressage is a discipline that rewards experience – or rather it did before Dujardin burst upon the scene. In 19 months she has gone from performing in her first grand prix (where she set a record for a British debut) to winning on the greatest stage of all. Along the way she has won a European team gold and broken the world record for a score in a grand prix special.

Dujardin was full of praise for her 10-year-old gelding Valegro. She produced him from a novice with the support of her trainer and mentor Carl Hester, who co-owns the horse with Roly Luard. 'He was brilliant,' she said of Valegro, nicknamed

Charlotte Dujardin had good cause to celebrate – an Olympic gold and a record-breaking dressage score.

Blueberry. 'He was a little tired at the end, which is why we made a small mistake, but he went out there and gave his all – he's the horse of a lifetime.'

With Dujardin the last into the arena, nerves were stretched taut. Anky van Grunsven, of the Netherlands, took an early lead but was swiftly overtaken by Helen Langehanenberg, of Germany.

Then Bechtolsheimer set the stadium alight with her programme; she thrilled the crowd with double canter pirouettes and half passes in passage. The applause had barely died down when Hester powered down the centre line on Uthopia in flamboyant style. Their piaffe and passage had enough artistic merit to compensate for the odd mistake but the mark of 82.857 per cent was not enough to reward him with an individual prize. Cornelissen then produced a sensational test to break the Olympic record with 88.250 per cent.

And then the moment of truth. Could Dujardin's fabled nerve hold? Familiar music rang out – piaffe to 'The Great Escape', walk to 'Land of Hope and Glory', canter pirouette to the chimes of Big Ben, all in perfect time – a mistake in the final pirouette – but then the halt and it was over.

The crowd screamed their admiration, Dujardin pointed to Blueberry as if to say: 'It's all him'. And everyone waited with bated breath for the score ...
– *Jenny MacArthur*

Keri-Anne Payne
Open-water marathon

Keri-Anne Payne was denied an Olympic medal because of thirst and a cruel half a second.

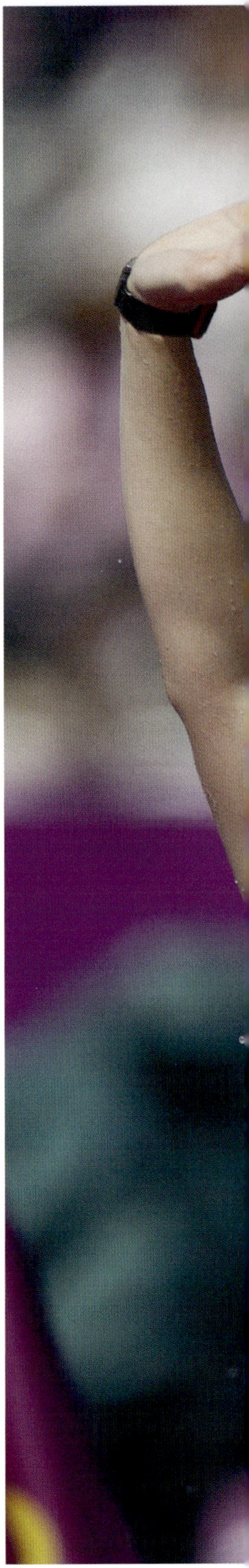

At Hyde Park, another British woman made a brave attempt to take gold, this time in the open-water marathon swim. But after nearly two hours, Keri-Anne Payne was denied her Olympic medal by less than half a second. After 10 kilometres, it was in the thrashing of tired limbs in the final few metres that Payne was denied, yet although this seemed one of the crueller so-near-yet-so-far failures, it was maybe a medal that she lost earlier in a fight over a drink.

It was also the last big gold medal hope for British Swimming. For that reason, pretty much the entire pool team had decamped to the banks of the Serpentine to cheer on their team-mate. Here was their world champion, their Beijing silver medal-winner, their get-out-of-jail card. No pressure, then, Keri-Anne.

This event is hard enough when you have to go 10 kilometres, but when you lob in being kicked and punched in the frothing swirl of rival swimmers, it is even harder. Some of the pack are well equipped to handle themselves in such company, but Payne declares herself 'more of a lover' than a fighter, one reason that she likes to leave the rest behind and dictate from the front.

The problem was that she was not alone. Eva Risztov, the Hungarian, is such a versatile swimmer that she competed in the 4 x 100 metres relay last week, an endurance athlete with a fast-twitch gene, but still not a natural candidate for grinding it out from the front. Risztov actually competed as far back as Sydney, at just 15; she was an old hand by the time Athens came round and there she found the disappointment of not reaching the podium so painful that she quit the sport. It was only with London in her sights that she was persuaded to give it one last throw.

She came to London with the clear intention of staying clear of the pack; it was a gamble to swim from the front, but one that she was prepared to take. And thus for much of the early part of the race she swum out ahead alongside Payne; they were so stroke-for-stroke close it seemed they were strapped together.

Payne never broke Risztov, nor could she shake Haley Anderson, the American who was an unknown quantity at this level, while old campaigners such as Martina Grimaldi, of Italy, also hung on, refusing to let her dictate. Payne could not therefore escape the pack and the war of attrition that goes with it. Yet she was in reasonable nick until she approached the third-lap feeding station.

At the point of the station, the swimmers want to be on the right-hand side of the pack, to be best positioned for the turn at the subsequent buoy, but the feed station was on the left. Had Payne been swimming out ahead solo, she would have been fine; however, in breaking left to the feed station, she hit the aggro. She first had to get past six swimmers to get to her bottle, but then when she reached to grab it, she missed, and in stopping to grab it again, the swimmers behind collided with her. This caused her to be 'disorientated', she said. 'I had no idea where I was going and had to work quite hard to get back up to positions I like to be in.' She added: 'I got hit a few times in the face and tried to deal with it as best as I could, but it took more energy out of me than I was expecting.'

It was in those moments that Risztov was able to go clear and after that, Payne struggled to get back to her. 'I probably could have got to her,' Payne said, 'but I'd have wasted too much energy.' She managed to remain, though, with a breakaway pack, four girls on the heels of Risztov.

Even in the last 100 metres, the race was on. Anderson edged up to Risztov but lost out, Payne edged up to Grimaldi to challenge for bronze but missed it, too. 'Open-water swimming is about who makes the right decisions,' Payne said afterwards. She conceded that the decision to go to that third-lap feed station was her 'error'. A small error, a massive what-if. She will never know what would have happened if she hadn't made it.

– Owen Slot

Men's team
Hockey

IT COULD TAKE more than 36 hours for Great Britain's traumatised players to recover from their humiliating 9–2 defeat at the hands of the Netherlands and pick themselves up for the bronze-medal play-off against Australia. Jason Lee, the head coach, said that he was embarrassed at the margin of the defeat, while Barry Middleton, the captain, said that all he could think of to say was 'sorry'.

Having gone into their first semi-final in 24 years with high hopes of emulating the golden days of Seoul in 1988, they were annihilated by the Dutch, who will meet Germany in the final.

The outcome was effectively decided in the first half, when the Netherlands displayed overwhelming superiority in pace and penetration to take a 4–1 lead.

Seizing on errors by GB, they clinically punished a hesitant defence that appeared in disarray for most of the opening exchanges. After a brief rally at the start of the second half, the home team were engulfed by wave after wave of orange.

Lee admitted that they had been slack early. 'At 3–1 and 4–1 down, we still believed we could win, but perhaps we were reckless too early,' Lee said. 'The upsetting thing is that we completely lost our game midway through the second half.'

Britain have not beaten the Netherlands since 2000 and it was going to take a superhuman effort to match the flair, vision and ball control of their opponents. Middleton was mystified as to where it had all gone wrong. 'We didn't turn up,' he said. 'It was one of the most disappointing days of my career.'

– *Cathy Harris*

Bolt, Blake and Weir
200 metres

Another great night in the Athletics Stadium for Jamaica, as Bolt, Blake and Weir run in to take gold, silver and bronze.

IF THE AUDIENCE for Super Saturday thought they had seen the Jamaicans do something special on the athletics track, the 200 metres final showed that the fastest man on Earth still had more to prove. The man who combines spellbinding sport, slacker cool, Swedish handball and parameter-pushing physicality, won again. Usain Bolt beat his friend and foe, Yohan Blake, to another gold medal and the world seemed all the better for it.

Bolt got out quickly and midway round the bend had a clear lead. Blake was three lanes inside him, second. It is testament to just how good Bolt is that he equalled Michael Johnson's old world record of 19.32 seconds to retain his title and it looked like high-class jogging.

'This is what I wanted,' he said. 'I've got it.' Blake has done his bit here, too. He clocked 19.44 seconds. That was the sixth best time in history. He went down fighting, but bullies do not come any less forgiving than Bolt. He has two golds and Blake two silvers – they are the most satisfying one-two combination in sport.

Warren Weir, another Jamaican, was third in 19.84 seconds. It was the first time that four men had dipped below 20 seconds in the same race.

Few sportsmen have adopted that air of couldn't-give-a-fig ambivalence to such positive effect. Bolt does not walk, he lopes. Not a natural walker, when he runs he drags half the world with him in a slipstream of snap-happy bliss. After crossing the line, Bolt celebrated with Blake and Weir. Incredibly, the three best 200 metres men in the world all train together on the same humble track in Kingston. Then Bolt took a camera off a photographer and started taking pictures himself.

Bolt has silenced every dissenting voice. Most people had stopped doubting Bolt and adopted the polar opposite position after his win on Super Saturday. Allan Wells, the 100 metres winner in 1980, was introduced to the crowd beforehand and said that nobody could beat Bolt. He obviously did not see the Jamaican trials, where Blake did just that.

The affection between Bolt and Blake, training and domino partners, is genuine. Theirs should be a dysfunctional relationship, as sporting rivals rarely train together. Perhaps Bolt knows that he has nothing to fear by helping Blake. He does it his own way, uniquely, on and off the track. Bolt can party with half the Swedish women's handball team and still do miracles. Stunning.
– Rick Broadbent

Day 14 Round Up

FOOTBALL
The United States secured a 2–1 victory over Japan in the Olympic women's final as Carli Lloyd's double gave her country a third successive gold medal and avenged last year's World Cup final defeat by the same opponents.

Canada secured the bronze medal by beating France 1–0.

CANOEING
Rachel Cawthorn missed out on a canoe sprint medal for the second time in two days when she came sixth in the K1 final.

Cawthorn, 23, from Guildford, who had finished fifth with the women's K4 crew, began the race strongly before falling behind.

CYCLING
Liam Phillips set his sights on a final place and a possible medal after advancing to the BMX semi-finals with a strong quarter-final showing. Phillips finished second to Connor Fields in the first three runs and now the 23-year-old from Burnham-on-Sea is eyeing progress to the last eight. 'It's just survival, it's getting to that final,' he said.

MEDAL TABLE

				T
1. USA	39	25	26	90
2. CHINA	37	24	19	80
3. GREAT BRITAIN	25	13	14	52
4. RUSSIA	12	21	23	56
5. SOUTH KOREA	12	7	6	25

ATHLETICS: MEN'S 200 METRE FINAL

Gold JAM

19.32

Silver JAM

19.44

Bronze JAM

19.84

JAMAICA
BOLT
WEIR

JAMAICA
BLAKE

I LIKE
MY BALLS
BRONZED

10.08.12
London 2012 Olympic Games
Day 15

Medals won by Team GB
Gold 0
Silver 2
Bronze 3

15

470 Class
Sailing

TEARS OF JOY and of sorrow fell at Weymouth, as two sets of British sailors celebrated and lamented their silver-medal success. It was a case of same medal, same boat but different reactions after they failed to turn a certain silver into gold.

For Luke Patience and Stuart Bithell, this was a silver medal won and they celebrated by laughing. Patience, a charismatic Scot, did a somersault into the water, while the slightly more reserved Bithell, from Rochdale, called for champagne.

For Hannah Mills and Saskia Clark, it was a gold medal lost. 'I'm still feeling a bit raw,' a tearful Mills said an hour after their race, having blown a good chance to add an Olympic title to the world title that they won three months ago.

The demands of the medal races were slightly different and the way they panned out goes some way to explaining the reactions. In both cases a silver was assured, but the men needed not only to beat Malcolm Page and Mathew Belcher, of Australia, but to finish with another boat between them. It was not wholly in their hands.

The British boat made a quicker start than Australia, but, with only Croatia going with the two leaders and a large gap developing to the rest, it became clear that Patience and Bithell would not get much help. In an attempt to bring more boats back into play, Bithell and Patience fought doggedly on the second upwind leg, tacking and twisting one way and the other to slow them and allow the rest to catch up. In the end, Australia managed to stay ahead, while Britain had to take a penalty turn for illegally pumping the boat to get more speed in the light wind.

Mills and Clark got caught on the wrong side of the course on the first upwind leg, found no wind there and watched New Zealand stretch away to a gold medal-winning lead. Their equation was more simple. With Britain and New Zealand level on points, it mattered only who finished first. They got away better but New Zealand suddenly tacked right sharply and, instead of going with them, Mills and Clark got stuck between the Australia and Italy boats. With New Zealand breaking away, they tried the left and fell victim to a big wind shift. New Zealand won by 2½ minutes.

'She [New Zealand] had a massive jump on us and suddenly there was a 200-metre lead,' Clark said. 'After a quarter of the race, it was all over and all we could do was watch the scrap for bronze.'
– *Patrick Kidd*

‘I wouldn’t want them to be anything other than gutted. If you haven’t got that feeling, you haven’t got a hope of winning gold.’
Stephen Park, Team Manager

For Hannah Mills and Saskia Clark, not even a silver medal was enough to get them out of the doldrums.

Women's team
Hockey

IT WAS NEVER going to be easy to lift themselves, but Great Britain's women's hockey team chose the right time to put together one of their best performances of the Games when they beat New Zealand on Day 15 to take the bronze medal.

Their 3–1 victory at the Riverbank Arena ended a 20-year wait to capture a medal and matches the bronze won by the women in Barcelona in 1992.

The squad had targeted gold in the countdown to the Olympics and admitted that they were devastated to lose in the semi-finals to Argentina, who took the silver medal after losing to the Netherlands. 'It hurt a lot,' Kate Walsh, the captain, said. 'But I knew when it came to game-day we would do it.'

Finishing with a medal represented a personal triumph for Walsh, who played with a protective face mask five days after having surgery to insert a titanium plate in her jaw, which she broke in the team's first match, against Japan.

Craig Parnham, the assistant coach and former Great Britain captain, said that Walsh was the team's inspiration, adding: 'What she did was huge. When you think she had a general anaesthetic, surgery, a plate, and drinks her meals through a straw, it's remarkable what she's achieved.'

New Zealand have been hailed as the tournament's surprise package after earning a place in the last four for the first time in four Olympic appearances. Coached by Mark Hager, the former Australia forward, they have risen up the world rankings to No 5, one below Britain. Three superbly executed penalty-corner goals in the second half settled the result in a hard-fought contest, with Britain showing superb organisation and commitment. Aggressive and tenacious after the break, they simply outplayed their opponents.

Walsh said that her team-mates never lost the desire to win a medal. 'We stayed in the bubble and they were never distracted, never lost their focus,' she said. 'We knew exactly what we had to do, and in between moments of intense concentration, I thought, "We're doing it, it's all going to plan."'

The most experienced member of the squad with 294 caps, Walsh is not making any immediate decisions about her future. 'I still love playing,' she said. 'It's hard to turn your back on something when you're still improving.'
– *Cathy Harris*

Lutalo Muhammad and Sarah Stevenson

Taekwondo

Lutalo Muhammad silenced those who doubted his place in the Olympics by winning bronze.

WITH SO MUCH at stake at an Olympic Games, the battle to qualify is one that tests the toughest of nerves. On Day 15, one of the great Olympic selection controversies ended in a dramatic home bronze, with Lutalo Muhammad, a 21-year-old from Walthamstow, dancing around the mat twirling the Union Jack above his head in joy, while simultaneously the familiar yet harsh question was being asked: was this a bronze won or a gold medal lost?

The question is deeply unfair on Muhammad, who found himself in the invidious position of being given the honour of representing his country while many said that he should not be.

The selectors had the opportunity to pick the European champion and world No 1, Aaron Cook, at this weight, yet went for the inexperienced 21-year-old, who is ranked No 59. The selection reeked of politics but the GB Taekwondo management insisted that Muhammad's ability to execute headkicks would be the difference.

It left Muhammad with an unfair weight of pressure upon his shoulders. He did win his first bout, but he lost the second to Nicolás García Hemme, 7–3, a bout in which he struggled to assert himself. But then he managed to recover and fought through another qualification fight, against Yousef Karami, of Iran, before he was lined up against Arman Yeremyan, of Armenia, for bronze.

His victory was also a success for the selectors because both his last two winning fights were settled by his special weapon, the headkick.

It was a disappointing day for Sarah Stevenson, who had travelled to the World Championships last year – and won – while her parents were fighting battles against cancer that they would both lose. Her Olympic campaign was then hampered by a knee injury that was so bad that there were doubts that she would be fit for these Games. Those doubts were quickly justified. In the first round, Stevenson was drawn against Paige McPherson and she went 3–0 down and never got on level terms, losing the bout 5–1. 'I wanted to win, I wanted to fight,' she said. 'You should be here to have fun, give it everything. That's what I did. My mum and dad would have wanted me to be here, they would have been proud.'
– Owen Slot

Men's team

4 x 400 metres relay

Adam Gemili clasps the baton all too late as Britain's relay team are disqualified.

On a day of mixed fortunes in the relays, Martyn Rooney ran a lustrous last leg for Team GB in the 4 x 400 metres final, but could not get into the medals.

Rooney gave it his all and Jack Green can be proud of his second-leg run, but it was the Bahamas team that took their first track gold from the United States of America. It was a race of raw passion and rich drama, but Dai Greene lost ground on the third leg and Rooney could not make amends. Cuba's hopes also faded when one of their athletes pulled a hamstring.

If Greene, who has endured a miserable Olympics, was downcast, the same went for Adam Gemili, the new sprint sensation, who formed part of the 4 x 100 metres team. It was unfortunate that the man responsible for an age-old problem should be Britain's new sensation. Gemili seemed to break too soon on the fourth leg and left the changeover zone without a baton. When he got it, he ran beautifully to finish second behind Jamaica, but he joined a long list of those responsible for cock-ups.

The pity is that the team, with Christian Malcolm and Dwain Chambers on the first two legs, looked quick enough to light up the final night. Their time was 37.93 seconds, which would have been their best for five years if it had stood.

'He rose to the occasion,' Malcolm said of Gemili, maintaining his glass-overflowing rather than half-empty outlook on calamity. 'He got his adrenalin going and he went out hard. If these guys can be in a team and run a 37.9 at that age, then it all bodes well.'

The past is not on the sprint relay team's side. This was the fourth out of five Games where the men's team has either dropped the baton or been disqualified. The exit of the team meant that the old and new bade farewell to unforgettable experiences. Gemili will be back for more, having run 10.05 seconds this summer, and with the second-fastest man in history, Tyson Gay, tipping him to be one of the all-time greats.
– Rick Broadbent

Day 15 Round Up

GYMNASTICS
Having successfully appealed against the decision by British Gymnastics not to nominate them, Great Britain's rhythmic gymnasts performed and finished twelfth and last in the group all-round qualification round.

SWIMMING
Oussama Mellouli became the first swimmer to win Olympic titles in pool and open water when he won the 10-kilometre marathon in 1 hour 49 minutes 55.1 seconds. The silver went to Thomas Lurz, of Germany, 3.4 seconds behind, and the bronze to Richard Weinberger, of Canada, 5.2 seconds from gold.

Daniel Fogg, the Briton, 25 this month and swimming only his fourth big 10-kilometre race, rallied to finish a worthy fifth.

BASKETBALL
The France women's basketball team face arguably the most futile task in these Olympics as they attempt to deny the United States a fifth successive gold medal. The US are now unbeaten in 20 years and 40 games, and hope to become the first nation in Olympic history to win five successive golds in a team sport.

MEDAL TABLE

				T
1. USA	41	26	27	94
2. CHINA	37	25	19	81
3. GREAT BRITAIN	25	15	17	57
4. RUSSIA	15	21	27	63
5. SOUTH KOREA	13	7	7	27

TOP NATIONS: SAILING MEDALS IN NUMBERS

AUS

3

(3G 0S 0B)

GBR

5

(1G 4S 0B)

NED

3

(1G 1S 1B)

11.08.12
London 2012 Olympic Games
Day 16

Medals won by Team GB
Gold 3
Silver 0
Bronze 1

16

Mo Farah
5,000 metres

Below: Farah and Bolt swap trademark poses in the Olympic Stadium.

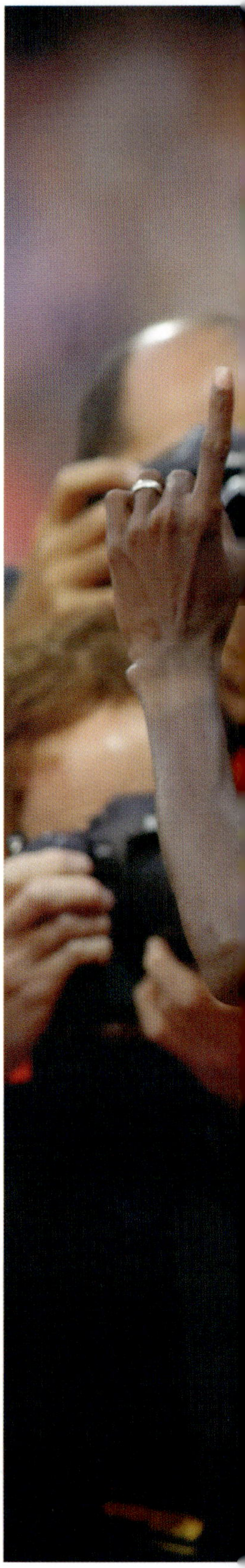

YOU CAN TALK about housing estates, obesity and a nascent love of handball, but the instant legacy of London 2012 is in the indelible memories. So when Mo Farah and Usain Bolt struck their poses on their shared podium at the end of the penultimate day of the competition, the deal was done. It was the snap seen around the world.

Jessica Ennis was the face of the Games, and she delivered, but Farah and Bolt are the tag-team that has wrestled the title from her. One did 50 laps and the other won three gold medals in 66 seconds. They are the long and short of Olympic running, two men, five titles, one image.

It was fitting that, after all the ceremonies, they stood on the podium together, Farah doing the lightning bolt 'to de world' pose, Bolt doing the 'Mobot'. It sums up the two men's influence on the sporting world. Bolt has long been an oddity who marries athletic excellence with parties, crashed cars, asides about Manchester United and all-round slacker shtick. Farah, too, likes to smile, watch Arsenal and exudes an air of utter enjoyment. Farah and Bolt are friends. They share a manager. After Farah crossed the line to complete the 10,000 and 5,000 metres double, he did a few sit-ups, aping Bolt's post-race press-ups after winning the 200 metres. Farah said. 'I can't believe he did the Mobot as he was breaking a world record.'

Farah was Europe's double distance champion and had the 5,000 metres world title, but eight days in London have taken him to another level. He produced a thrilling finale to the athletics programme, and by completing the long-distance double he underlined his status as the finest endurance runner in the world. Farah's win gave Great Britain their fourth athletics gold, a figure they have managed only twice since 1920.

What he does next is likely to be down to his coach. It is another trait he shares with Bolt. Both men are utterly deferential to their mentors and have total faith in them. Farah moved to the United States last year to work with Alberto Salazar, a Cuban-born coach whose pulse once stopped for 14 minutes. Technically, he died, but now he has breathed fresh life into British sport.
– Rick Broadbent

London 2012
1808
3

Luke Campbell
Boxing

Luke Campbell acknowledges the cheers of the crowd as he wins Olympic gold.

THERE WERE tears all round at the ExCel Centre as Luke Campbell won the bantamweight gold medal, although Fred Evans had to settle for silver at welterweight.

Campbell dazzled on his biggest night, as he won with an almost punch-perfect display of back-foot boxing. The 24-year-old from Hull beat John Joe Nevin 14–11 on points in the final. If that sounds close, it wasn't. Campbell simply beat the Irishman to the punch throughout the three rounds.

He kept the bout at range, let Nevin make mistakes and counter-punched brilliantly, knocking him down in the final round. 'It was a very difficult fight, very technical, because we knew each other very well,' Campbell said. 'He's a top, top fighter. It was all about outwitting each other. The plan was just to keep moving from side to side and let the punches go.'

In 2008, Campbell became the first British boxer in nearly half a century to win a European gold medal. But he then struggled, falling out of favour with those running the squad and then being sidelined with a hand injury.

'It was a very low point for me,' Campbell said. 'I had my best year ever in 2008 and then the system changed, new coaches came in and the whole of 2009 was just a misery for me.

'There was a point where I wanted to get out, I just didn't want to box any more, because I didn't like the environment I was in. Then Rob McCracken came in [as performance director] and changed things with the coaches and took me under his wing.'

– *Ron Lewis*

Ed McKeever

200 metre canoe sprint

On a day of three golds for Team GB, one was all the more remarkable for the fact that it might never have happened.

There is much that the success of Ed McKeever tells us about the Olympics, but greatest of all is how random is this gargantuan sporting festival. Athletes' success can rise and fall on the back of decisions made by lobbyists and committee rooms. The first time the Games came to London, they had tug of war, but there is no event for tug-of-war specialists to enter now. In Beijing four years ago there was a baseball competition, but that has gone now, too. And but for the whim of the International Canoe Federation (ICF), we would probably never have heard of McKeever, the 28-year-old from Bradford on Avon who dresses his dog in an Olympic scarf.

The dog is a bit of a sidetrack here, although but for the ICF, we would not know about him either. The point is that, before these Games, flatwater Olympic canoeing only involved 500 metre and 1,000 metre races. In other words, middle-distance events. Sprinters did not get a look in. Until 2009, there was no 200 metres canoe sprint. Until then, McKeever was desperately trying to make it as a middle-distancer but not managing it.

The transformation of McKeever into a sprinter required a total change in stroke rate. Over 1,000 metres, paddlers move at a rate of about 110 strokes per minute; for 200 metre, McKeever increased his to 160. The speed of each stroke is critical, too.

In a 200 metre race, the start is clearly a key factor. As Purcell said, this is where McKeever is special. 'He is a little bit unique,' he said, 'in that at his start, he takes one of the longest strokes of anyone in the world. He can just hold himself in that position, lock himself and move the boat.'

There is another detail in all this and his name is Ed Cox. He is not in the GB team because McKeever is. However, McKeever needed Cox. He trains better when he has someone to race, and he always trains with and races Cox. During the first week of the Games, the sprint canoeists were preparing at a camp in Barcelona. Cox went dutifully to train with, race with, and get beaten by McKeever.

McKeever's story is one of the perfect athlete with the perfect temperament and the perfect training partner. And but for the whim of the ICF, we might never have heard it.

– Owen Slot

Little-known Ed McKeever makes his name in the 200 metre canoe sprint and takes top spot on the winners' podium.

2
MCKEEVER E.
NELO

Tom Daley
Individual diving

In a diving final that had the spectators' emotions twisting and turning as much as the divers, Tom Daley satisfied everyone with a well-earned bronze.

If LONDON 2012 has all been about great expectations, no one felt them as keenly as Tom Daley, the teenage diving sensation.

When Daley was 12, he sat in his bedroom at home in Plymouth and drew his dream. Beneath the words 'my ambition' was a diver doing a handstand on the 10-metre board, with the Olympic rings and 'London 2012' on either side.

Those symbols, engraved on the bottom of the pool, were the last thing the 18-year-old saw before taking flight to a bronze medal in the 10-metre platform final at the Aquatics Centre.

'On the last dive, I looked down at the pool and my eye-line was exactly where those London 2012 Olympic rings are,' Daley said. 'I was staring at the floor at those [symbols]. It doesn't get any more pressurised than that. I thought: "It's do or die." I had to give it all I had.'

For the youngest European champion, aged 13, in 2008, the baby of Team GB in Beijing at 14 and the youngest world champion at 15, winning the first individual diving medal for Britain since 1960 was a dream come true for the youngster – who had the nation on the edge of their seats.

Daley took a slim lead – 466.05 to 466.20 – over Qiu Bo, the favourite from China, and David Boudia, of the United States, in the fifth round. A final 3½ somersault from Daley drew two 9s and a 9.5, leaving him with a total of 556.95 and the No 1 by his name. Boudia was next on the board, his advantage a dive with a higher tariff. Gold for Daley was gone as Boudia moved to 568.65; Qiu bowed out bruised on 566.85 for silver.

'For me, getting bronze was something I'd worked so hard for since I was a young kid,' said Daley. Letting his ambitions slip out, he added: 'I wanted to win gold . . . er, to win a medal, since I started out and Olympic gold is an achievement I will aim for at an upcoming Games. I got bronze. It was a solid performance. I'm just over the moon to have come away with an Olympic medal.'

Scenes of jubilation followed Daley's success, the entire Britain team leaping together into the pool. Daley rushed over to Debbie, his mother, and his brothers, and dedicated the medal to his father, Rob, who died of cancer last year. 'I really wish my dad was here to see me do that performance because we had such a long, tough journey together.'

– Craig Lord

'I really wish my dad was here to see me do that performance because we had such a long, tough journey together.'

Men's team
4 x 100 metres relay

The 'greatest track meeting in history' came to an end with the 'greatest athlete to live' producing another world record. How fitting that it should be Usain Bolt who ran the final 100 metres of a coruscating programme.

Bolt stormed down the strip of track that he has been scorching along all week to give Jamaica the 4 x 100 metres relay gold. The time of 36.85 seconds seemed barely feasible and took 0.19 seconds off the mark the same quartet set at last summer's World Championships.

The United States, who had fancied their chances of upstaging Jamaica in this event, were second, Bolt destroying Ryan Bailey on the anchor leg. The American team, including Tyson Gay and Justin Gatlin, equalled the old world record of 37.04 seconds.

Bolt, who had labelled himself 'the greatest' after his 200 metres win, thus completing the Olympic double, leaves London with three golds and one world record. Not bad for a man who said he was only 90 per cent fit and had accepted that he would never be a fast starter.

It was the fastest finish to a meeting that Lord Coe had termed 'the greatest'. London can feel smugly satisfied that it saw Bolt in his pomp. If he does make it to Rio in 2016, it is hard to imagine he will be quicker then than now. London may have been his Olympic farewell, PT Barnum in spikes ruling the five-ringed circus for the last time.

The only thing to sour his and the crowd's mood was when an official insisted on taking the baton off him. Bolt wanted it, either as a souvenir or to give to a fan as a memento, and having already complained about the endless rules at these Olympics, he looked momentarily displeased. Later, in a good PR move, he got it back.

– Rick Broadbent

Day 16 Round Up

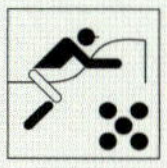

PENTATHLON
In the men's pentathlon, David Svoboda, of the Czech Republic, won the gold medal. He won 26 of his bouts in fencing, slipped back after a poor swim but kept Cao Zhongrong, of China, at bay over the run. Nick Woodbridge and Sam Weale, of Great Britain, were tenth and thirteenth.

ATHLETICS
United States win the women's 4 x 400 metres relay. Keshorn Walcott won gold for Trinidad and Tobago in the men's javelin.

Anna Chicherova won the women's high jump for Russia.

FOOTBALL
Mexico surprised Brazil to win men's football gold at Wembley, with a final score of 2–1.

MEDAL TABLE

				T
1. USA	42	29	29	100
2. CHINA	38	26	21	85
3. GREAT BRITAIN	28	15	18	61
4. RUSSIA	21	25	32	78
5. SOUTH KOREA	13	7	7	27

DIVING: 10 METRE PLATFORM FINAL

Gold USA

568.65

Silver CHN

566.85

Bronze GBR

556.95

London 2012
London 2012
London 2012
adidas

12.08.12
London 2012 Olympic Games
Day 17

Medals won by Team GB
Gold 1
Silver 2
Bronze 1

17

Anthony Joshua

Boxing

WITH JUST a few hours until the closing ceremony of London 2012, Anthony Joshua won Team GB's last gold medal, bringing the home team's boxing medal tally to an impressive three golds, one silver and one bronze.

Anthony Joshua's telephone will be ringing with offers to become an instant millionaire. The boxer insists he will sit at home in Golders Green, ignore the siren call and nurse his gold medal in his giant hands.

No Olympic hero has a better opportunity to turn gold into hard cash than a champion boxer – especially a 6ft 6in, 18st heavyweight – and Joshua could be straight on a flight to the United States to seek his fortune. Yet he is adamant that he will not succumb to temptations to leave the amateur ranks after his superheavyweight triumph.

'It was never about money,' he said, insisting that he could get by just fine on his Lottery funding of about £30,000. It is, he says, about learning, about developing as an amateur, about becoming a world champion. 'Money won't be hard to resist,' he said. 'I've got bills to pay, but to leave something so great as the GB set-up because of money would be a big mistake. I don't want to lose that because money is thrown in my face.'

He has been boxing for only four years but has learnt so much, some from painful experience. Having admitted possession of herbal cannabis two years ago and been forced to tend allotments for his community service, his career might have been over before it had started. But he knuckled down.

Anthony Joshua celebrates his boxing final win over Italian Roberto Cammarelle to take Britain's last Olympic gold of the London 2012 Games.

Even in the euphoria of victory, he was talking with admirable perspective. Gold mattered to him, 'for representing my journey, my suffering as well as the triumph'. But he added: 'I don't think a gold medal makes a man.'

Joshua cannot remember what he was doing four years ago. He knows only that he owes a big debt of thanks to the cousin who persuaded him to come down to Finchley Amateur Boxing Club to relieve teenage boredom. 'He lent me 25 quid for some Lonsdale boots and I borrowed some shorts,' Joshua said. And now he is Olympic champion and one of the hottest amateur prospects around.

Joshua insists that his focus is on the World Championships next year and the Commonwealth Games in Glasgow in 2014. 'I've got a lot to learn,' he says. 'I'm in no rush. These memories are priceless, coming to the Olympics, winning gold.'
– *Matt Dickinson*

Fred Evans
Boxing

Above: Fred Evans gave it his best shot in the welterweight final, coming through with a silver medal for Team GB.

EARLIER IN the final day, another British boxer fought to the last as he battled for gold in the welterweight final. In the end, after a valiant effort, Fred Evans claimed a silver after losing 17–9 to Serik Sapiyev, a former double world champion from Kazakhstan.

The 21-year-old Welshman had an incredible run to the final, winning four bouts, including a semi-final victory over Taras Shelestyuk, the world No 1 from Ukraine. But against Sapiyev, Evans just seemed to run out of steam and ideas.

Sapiyev started quickly, but Evans just could not get a foothold in the bout, as the Kazakh peppered him with shots. He tried to mix it in the last, but Sapiyev was in total control. 'I've had four hard fights, this was my fifth and he was just sharper,' Evans said. 'I couldn't get things going. I'm still young and over the moon at getting to the final.'
– *Ron Lewis*

Samantha Murray
Modern pentathlon

The shooting event rounded off a tough modern pentathlon for Samantha Murray and secured her a silver medal.

AS THE SUN began to set on the Games, Samantha Murray ran into the Greenwich Park arena to an enormous cheer and sealed Britain's 65th and final Olympic medal.

After the hept, dec and triathletes, it was finally the turn of the modern pentathletes. The pentathlon is almost a greatest hits of what went before, with a little bit of fighting, athletics, pool and horsey action to remind everyone of what they will miss when they return to work. British women have always done well at such multitasking, but few expected Murray, 22, to be on the podium half an hour into the day. She lost her first seven fights with the epée, but soared back into contention in the pool and finally moved up to second place on the last lap of the 3-kilometre run that ended the day.

First up, the fencing, in which each of the 36 competitors takes on the 35 others in a series of one-minute, first-hit-wins contests. Murray had a disastrous start but finished mid-table with 18 wins and 17 losses. Team GB's Mhairi Spence, world champion in Rome this year, was only one win better off.

Murray got back into the competition with the second fastest 200-metre swim in Olympic history. Her time of 2 minutes 8.20 seconds was only 0.09 seconds slower than Sarolta Kovacs, of Hungary, recorded in the same heat, and lifted her up to third overall.

It was on, then, to Greenwich for the remaining disciplines, starting with 12 fences of showjumping. The athletes were given their horses at random, drawn from a champagne bucket, and had only 20 minutes to get to know their mount. After such equine speed dating, there were inevitably some awkward fumbles and riders being thrown from the saddle. The only rider to jump clear was Iryna Khokhlova, of Ukraine. Spence, riding a dappled silver steed named Coronado's Son, clonked four fences to slip to twelfth overall, but luck smiled on Murray, who hit two fences without dislodging the bars but did knock over the two obstacles celebrating Charles Darwin and the Post Office.

The day finished with a combined running and shooting event. The cross-country course was 3,000 metres and before each kilometre the athlete had to shoot a laser pistol at a target 10 metres away and get five hits. Murray was sixth after the first round of shooting but made up three places on the first lap and, with Yane Marques of Brazil looking wobbly, put in a sprint after the third round to take second place.
– Patrick Kidd

adidas
TEAM GB
London 2012
EAT BRITAI
MURRAY
KHOKHLOVA

United States v Spain
Basketball final

LONDON 2012 has proved itself to be an Olympics for the ages and, in keeping with the theme of the past two weeks, the United States and Spain produced a match worthy of the occasion before the gold-medal favourites prevailed by seven points.

David Stern, the all-powerful NBA Commissioner who has whispered of removing his league's players from future Olympics because of fears of injury and fatigue, sat in the area reserved for dignitaries. If basketball, in northern Europe at least, is a game with which the rank-and-file sports fan struggles to identify, the packed, multicultural international crowds that have watched in London speak of the global popularity of the game. All of which makes the potential loss of the world's best players from the Olympics all the more baffling.

Thankfully, the noises from USA Basketball, the national governing body, and Fiba, the association of national organisations governing international competitions, have become more conciliatory over the past week.

The arguments could be put aside as some of the NBA's finest – Spain boast eight players past and present from that league – put on a stunning display. For, ignore that notorious 1972 Munich final when the USSR were allowed to beat the USA by blatantly biased officiating, and this was the closest-fought final in Olympic history.

Juan Carlos Navarro played exceptionally well in the first period, scoring 14 points as Spain built a surprising five-point lead that forced the US into a 35–25 advantage. But the US long-distance shooting soon dried up, Spain's improved, through Rudy Fernández and Sergio Rodríguez, while brothers Pau and Marc Gasol punished the US close to the basket as the lead changed hands a good half dozen times.

Kevin Durant scored important three-pointers late in the third and Paul opened the fourth with five straight points that extended the US lead to six points. With Durant finishing on 30 points and leading lights LeBron James (19) and Bryant (17) providing important baskets, the United States were able to win their 62nd international from the past 63. With the US women having extended their Olympic winning streak to 40 games in winning gold against France, the only challenge to the US men's claim to be the best basketball team in the world probably comes from within its own borders.

– Ian Whitell

LeBron James and his United States team-mates battled to win gold and to prove themselves the best basketball team in the world.

Day 17 Round Up

ATHLETICS
Stephen Kiprotich of Uganda, stunned the Kenyan challenge to clinch a surprise Olympic gold medal in the marathon on The Mall and claim only Uganda's second Olympic gold medal in athletics. Kiprotich crossed the line in 2 hours 8 minutes 1 second, 26 seconds ahead of Kirui, the world champion, with Kipsang, the winner of the London Marathon this year, a further 1 minute 10 seconds behind.

Lee Merrien, of Britain, finished 30th in 2:17:00 and his team-mate, Scott Overall, was 61st in 2:22:37.

WATER POLO
Croatia secured their first men's water polo Olympic gold medal with an 8–6 victory over Italy.

HANDBALL
France have written themselves into the history books after becoming the first country to retain the Olympic title in men's handball after a nervy 22–21 victory over Sweden in the final. Les Bleus, who won gold in Beijing four years ago and are also the world champions, survived a late comeback by Sweden to take gold.

VOLLEYBALL
Russia became the first team in the history of men's Olympic volleyball to win the final from two sets down as they stunned Brazil at Earls Court. Russia lost the first two sets 25–19, 25–20, but roared back to take the last three sets 29–27, 25–22, 15–9 for the title.

WRESTLING
A wrestler who was taken to hospital by ambulance after his heart started racing during a quarter-final defeat got up from his bed and returned to win a bronze medal. Khetag Gazyumov, 29, from Azerbaijan, left the wrestling mat in a wheelchair after his heart-rate soared to a dangerous 260 beats per minute, compared with a normal rate of 60 to 100 but decided to return to the Games when he heard that he had earned a place in the bronze-medal play-off. He comfortably beat Rustam Iskandari, of Tajikistan, and Reza Yazdani, of Iran, to win bronze.

MEDAL TABLE

				T
1. USA	46	29	29	104
2. CHINA	38	27	23	88
3. GREAT BRITAIN	29	17	19	65
4. RUSSIA	24	26	32	82
5. SOUTH KOREA	13	8	7	28

TOTAL WORLD RECORDS

28

TOTAL OLYMPIC RECORDS

53

17 days later

Simon Barnes

OUR REVELS now are ended, but the past 17 days have been such stuff as dreams are made of. The London Olympic Games have ended and the greatest party in the history of the world is now a memory. Or a raft of them.

Looks like we got away with it, then. Looks like London 2012 was – well, we don't really go in for boasting in this country, but it was, shall we say, not bad. Really quite good, in fact. Quite good for us: rest of the world, was it good for you, too? It was, you know. I think a nation can tell.

London got it right. That's the big thing. London got it right for many complex organisational reasons, but ultimately because suddenly, everybody wanted to get it right. It was a 17-day *amour fou* of mad passion and deep fulfilment. It ended with a loud, noisy, flashy popfest with a lot of jokes thrown in: appropriate touches of wit, eccentricity, invention and self-mocking humour.

People came to the Games from all over the world and had a good time. People bantered in the queues and the trains. Volunteers smiled and told them where the lavs were and really quite often pointed in the right direction. The squaddies cleared up someone else's cock-ups and they did the tedious security job with colossal good nature. In the venues it was all couples and families, no gangs of blokes, no boozy aggression, no tribalism. Plenty of Last-Night-of-the-Proms patriotism, but there was also respect for the winners even when they came from abroad.

The national will to make the Games a success brought about a few quiet miracles, and the first of these was the weather. After the wettest April, May and June since Noah, the sun came out. Right from the first, this felt like a lucky Games, as if God had turned up and was in the mood for a bit of sport. The second miracle brought about by the will of the people was the vast collection of British medals. Again and again, British competitors found themselves in the startling position of playing better, running faster, throwing farther than they ever had before. Extra strength and ability came in the gift of this sudden love for the Games and the explosion of national will to make them succeed.

Savour that medal count: 65 in total, 29 of them gold, putting Britain into third place in the medal

The greatest party in London came to an end in a celebration of British music and eccentricity.

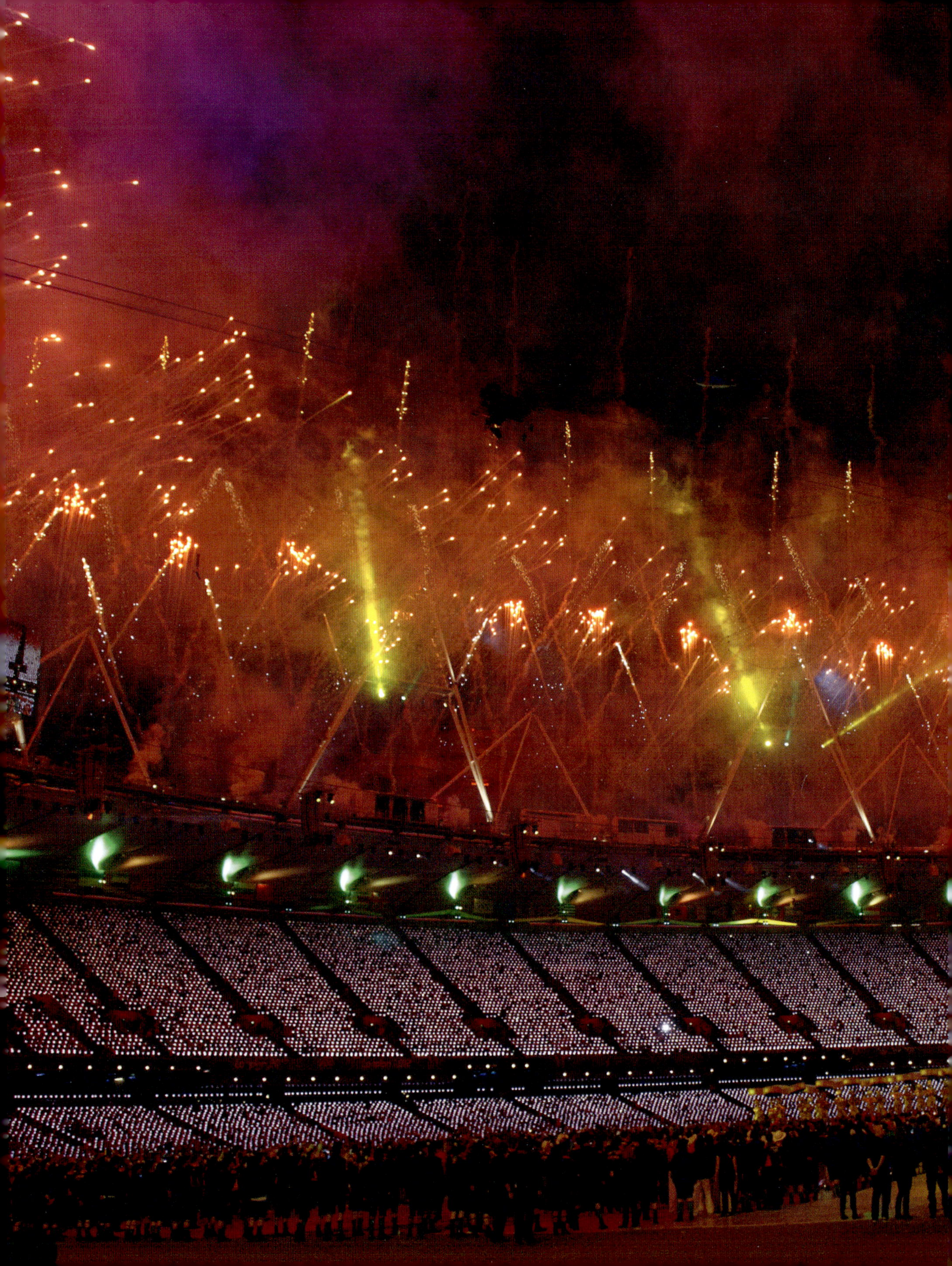

Fireworks filled the stadium with colour, on a night when the Olympic flame in the cauldron was extinguished to mark the end of the Games.

table, behind the United States and China, ahead of Russia, miles and miles ahead of poor old Australia. Gold in athletics, gold in rowing, gold in yachting, gold in shooting, gold in all kinds of glorious and obscure disciplines and, glory be, two golds in dressage.

We embraced the Games in all their demented diversity. And perhaps it was also the national will that brought great performances from international superstars: Michael Phelps winning his 18th gold, David Rudisha setting a world record in the 800 metres, Allyson Felix bagging three golds on the track and, of course, the ineffable Usain Bolt.

The sights and sounds and spirit of London filled the Games: horses jumping off Greenwich Hill more or less straight into Canary Wharf, marathon runners turning wearily into The Mall, cyclists going for a day-trip to Box Hill, beach volleyball under the Queen's windowsill, Wimbledon, Lord's, the Renoir scene at the Serpentine as the long-distance swimmers churned the water into Impressionist colours.

There was also a very London, a very English mood to the Games. They were never without humour or a touch of self-deprecation, a mood that continued into the closing ceremony with its Robin Reliant and Michael Caine telling us once again: 'You're only supposed to blow the bloody doors off.' All the same, this was a celebration without apology, without guilt.

The colonial past made us who we are – people of the muddled multicultural present. The British once tried to take over the world. Now the world has taken over Britain and we are richer as a result. We cheered ourselves daft for a man called Mohamed, adored a little black female boxer from Leeds and made a national saint of Jessica Ennis.

What was your favourite bit? That was everybody's favourite question in the cheery end-of-term mood in the Olympic Stadium. What was mine? All of it, of course. It's like choosing your favourite bit of a balloon: cut it out from the rest and you haven't got a balloon any more. The Games are about totality, inclusivity and the biodiversity of humankind, and that was the London Olympics of 2012. So seven years of pre-Games complaints ended. No doubt there'll now be 77 years of whining about cost and legacy and Was It Really Worth It?

Bloody hell, it was worth it. It was all worth it for 17 days of glory and beauty and wonder and unity and madness and joy. And we were there, every one of us.

Credits

While every effort has been made to trace the owners of copyright material reproduced herein and secure permissions, the publishers would like to apologise for any omissions and will be pleased to incorporate missing acknowledgements in any future edition of this book.

p5: (Tower Bridge cover) Press Association; p6: (Flyover cover) Getty; p6: (Table Tennis cover) Getty; p6: (Bolt 100m cover) AFP; p6: (Nicola Adams cover) Action Images; p6: (Opening Ceremony cover) Marc Aspland/NI Syndication; p6: (Wiggins cover) Graham Hughes/ NI Syndication; p6: (Bolt cover) Marc Aspland/NI Syndication; p6: (Bolt 200m cover) Reuters; p7: (Lizzie Armitstead cover) Bradley Ormesher/NI Syndication; p7: (Canoe Slalom cover) ProSport; p7: (Equestrian cover) Kit Houghton; p7: (Synchronised Swimming cover) Empics; p7: (Gymnastics cover) Getty; p7: (Cycling cover) Getty; p7: (Chris Hoy cover) Marc Aspland/NI Syndication; p7: (Marathon cover) Imagosportfoto; p9: (Closing Ceremony cover) Getty; p10: (Opening Ceremony dance) Marc Aspland/NI Syndication; p12: (Opening Ceremony Industrial Revolution) Jamie McPhilimey/NI Syndication; p13: (Opening Ceremony chimney) Scott Hornby/ NI Syndication; p14: (Opening Ceremony Team GB) Marc Aspland/NI Syndication; p15: (Opening Ceremony rings) Marc Aspland/ NI Syndication; p16: (Opening Ceremony NHS) Marc Aspland/NI Syndication; p17: (Opening Ceremony – The torch) Marc Aspland/ NI Syndication; p18: (Road Cycling) Graham Hughes/NI Syndication; p21: (Men's Road Race) Graham Hughes/NI Syndication; p22-23: (Men's Road Race) Graham Hughes/NI Syndication; p24: (Michael Phelps) Scott Hornby/NI Syndication; p26: (Rebecca Adlington) Bradley Ormesher/NI Syndication; p28: (Lizzie Armitstead) Bradley Ormesher/NI Syndication; p29: (Rebecca Adlington – Medal) Marc Aspland/NI Syndication; p30-31: (Women's Road Race) Bradley Ormesher/NI Syndication; p32-33: (Beth Tweddle and Hannah Whelan) Lee Thompson/NI Syndication; p34: (Women's Gymnastics Team) Lee Thompson/NI Syndication; p36: (Daniel Purvis) Jamie McPhilimey/NI Syndication; p38: (GB gymnasts looking at medal) Scott Hornby/NI Syndication; p38: (Louis Smith) Jamie McPhilimey/ NI Syndication ; p39: (Daniel Purvis) Marc Aspland/NI Syndication; p40: (Synchronised Diving) Bradley Ormesher/NI Syndication; p40: (Zoe Smith) Jamie McPhilimey/NI Syndication; p41: (Gemma Spofforth) Graham Hughes/NI Syndication; p41: (Gemma Spofforth) Graham Hughes/NI Syndication; p42: (Liam Tancock watches USA celebrate) Graham Hughes/NI Syndication; p44: (Beth Tweddle) Paul Rogers/NI Syndication; p46: (Mary King) Paul Edwards/NI Syndication; p47: (Beth Tweddle) Paul Rogers/NI Syndication; p48-49: (Michael Phelps) Graham Hughes/NI Syndication; p50: (Phelps celebrating) Richard Pelham/NI Syndication; p52: (Wiggo fan) Graham Hughes/NI Syndication; p54-55: (GB Men's 8) Scott Hornby/NI Syndication; p56-57: (Bradley Wiggins) Richard Pelham/NI Syndication; p58: (Michael Jamieson) Jamie McPhilimey/NI Syndication; p60: (Men's Team Sprint – Chris Hoy, Philip Hindes, Jason Kelly) Marc Aspland/NI Syndication; p62: (Cycling – Chris Hoy) Marc Aspland/NI Syndication; p63: (Chris Hoy) Marc Aspland/NI Syndication; p64-65: (Peter Wilson – shooting) Scott Hornby/NI Syndication; p66: (Men's Double Canoe) Jamie McPhilimey/NI Syndication; p67: (Stott & Baillie) Jamie McPhilimey/NI Syndication; p68: (Rowing – Men's Fours) Lee Thompson/NI Syndication; p69: (Gemma Gibbons) Paul Edwards/NI Syndication; p70: (Victoria Pendleton) Richard Pelham/NI Syndication; p72: (Jessica Ennis feet) Graham Hughes/NI Syndication; p74: (Women's rowing) Jamie McPhilimey/NI Syndication; p75: (Alan Campbell) Bradley Ormesher/NI Syndication; p76-77: (Clancy, Thomas, Burke and Kennaugh) Getty; p78: (Rebecca Adlington) Bradley Ormesher/NI Syndication; p79: (Karina Bryant) Dan Charity/NI Syndication; p80: (Jessica Ennis) Graham Hughes/NI Syndication; p82-83: (Jessica Ennis) Marc Aspland/NI Syndication; p84: (Michael Phelps) Bradley Ormesher/NI Syndication; p86: (Mo Farah) Marc Aspland/NI Syndication; p88: (Rowing – Men's Fours) Jamie McPhilimey/NI Syndication; p89: (Women's Rowing) Jamie McPhilimey/NI Syndication; p91: (Women's Cycling) Bradley Ormesher/NI Syndication; p92: (Jessica Ennis) Graham Hughes/NI Syndication; p94-95: (Greg Rutherford) Richard Pelham/NI Syndication; p97: (Mo Farah) Scott Hornby/NI Syndication; p98: (Mo Farah & Greg Rutherford) Richard Pelham/NI Syndication; p100: (Christine Ohuruogu) Graham Hughes/NI Syndication; p102-3: (Andy Murray) Bradley Ormesher/NI Syndication; p104-5: (Ben Ainslie) Darren Fletcher/ NI Syndication; p106-7: (Christine Ohuruogu) Marc Aspland/NI Syndication; p108: (Louis Smith) Paul Rogers/NI Syndication; p108-9: (Max Whitlock) Jamie McPhilimey/NI Syndication; p109: (Gymnastics – Louis & Max) Jamie McPhilimey/NI Syndication; p110-11: (Usain Bolt) Marc Aspland/NI Syndication; p112: (Cycling – Ed Clancy) PA; p114: (Nicola Adams) Bradley Ormesher/NI Syndication; p117: (Cycling – Jason Kenny) Graham Hughes/NI Syndication; p118-19: (Cycling – Jason Kenny leads) Graham Hughes/NI Syndication; p121: (Team Showjumping – gold) Scott Hornby/NI Syndication; p122: (Beth Tweddle) Dan Charity/NI Syndication; p123: (Anthony Ogogo) Graham Hughes/NI Syndication; p124: (Kirani James) EPA; p126: (Dressage) Paul Rogers/NI Syndication; p128-9: (Chris Hoy) Marc Aspland/NI Syndication; p130-1: (Women's Cycling) Marc Aspland/NI Syndication; p132: (Cycling – Brownlee brothers) Graham Hughes/ NI Syndication; p133: (Alistair Brownlee) Graham Hughes/NI Syndication; p134-5: (Victoria Pendleton) Marc Aspland/NI Syndication; p136: (Robert Grabarz) Graham Hughes/NI Syndication; p138: (Liu Xiang) Associated Press; p140: (Lawrence Clarke) Bradley Ormesher/ NI Syndication; p142-3: (Women's Hockey) Jamie McPhilimey/NI Syndication; p144: (Allyson Felix) Bradley Ormesher/NI Syndication; p146: (Jade Jones) Paul Rogers/NI Syndication; p148-9: (Jade Jones) Paul Rogers/NI Syndication; p150-1: (Nicola Adams) Marc Aspland/NI Syndication; p152: (Dressage crowd) Paul Rogers/NI Syndication; p153: (Dressage) Paul Rogers/NI Syndication; p155: (Keri-Anne Payne) Marc Aspland/NI Syndication; p156: (Usain Bolt) Marc Aspland/NI Syndication; p158-9: (Men's 200m final) Marc Aspland/NI Syndication; p160: (Crowd) Dan Charity/NI Syndication; p162-3: (Women's Sailing) Darren Fletcher/NI Syndication; p164-5: (Lutalo Muhammad) Bradley Ormesher/NI Syndication; p166: (Adam Gemili – relay) Press Association; p168: (Tom Daley) Peter Tarry/NI Syndication; p170: (Mo Farah & Usain Bolt) Richard Pelham/NI Syndication; p171: (Mo Farah) Lee Thompson/NI Syndication; p172-3: (Luke Campbell) Press Association; p174-5: (Ed McKeever) Jamie McPhilimey/NI Syndication; p176-7: (Tom Daley) Peter Tarry/NI Syndication; p178: (Jamaica relay team) Lee Thompson/NI Syndication; p180: (Anthony Joshua) Bradley Ormesher/NI Syndication; p182: (Anthony Joshua) Bradley Ormesher/NI Syndication; p183: (Fred Evans) Bradley Ormesher/NI Syndication; p184-5: (Samantha Murray) Press Association; p186: (LeBron James) Marc Aspland/NI Syndication; p188-9: (Closing Ceremony phoenix) Susannah Ireland/NI Syndication; p190-1: (Closing Ceremony fireworks) Arthur Edwards/NI Syndication